Advance Praise

Navigating the Maze: Simple, Smarter Strategies to Fast-track Success is a breezy read, filled with anecdotes, short stories, and scenarios that aid young professionals in navigating the trials of working life.

—*Dr Shashi Tharoor, MP (INC), Author,*
Politician and Former International Civil Servant

This is an outstanding book on the alchemy of success in a turbulent world. Distilled from decades of experience in the corporate maze, the book delivers clear and practical clues to improve the quality of both work and life. Written by two exceptional thinkers of the interaction between the individual and the organization, this is an excellent read for anyone wanting to appreciate the fine art of balancing the inner drives and external pressures. Written in an easy style, the book entertains with stories while it demystifies the complex relationship between life and work. It is a book for these times.

—*Firdose Vandrevala, President AIMA,*
Former Executive Vice Chairman Essar Steel,
Dy. MD Tata Steel and MD Tata Power

With this book, Bharatji and Savitaji have brought together their rich experience into a very simple and easy (a rare combination!) practical guide that addresses all the different aspects of work-life with inspirational anecdotes and stories. The question–answer approach to presenting workplace secrets in a very analytical way is a sure guide (for any aspirant of success) to joy and well-being, while remaining free from stress.

—*Br Prasanna Swaroopa, Spiritual Seeker*

Books come in all shapes and sizes. Some discuss and share such complicated aspects that it takes a few reads of the same text to make sense of what is being communicated. And then there are others like the one written by Savita and Bharat which from their very inception are easy to grasp and understand. *Navigating the Maze: Simple, Smarter Strategies to Fast-track Success* is exactly what its name communicates. Seemingly deceptive on account of the simple language which has been used to communicate rather complex ideas and thoughts, this text is heavily laden with critical information that is key to achieving success. Each sentence has a meaning and intent and builds on the previous one to put forth comprehensive ideas that act as building blocks to success. What this book does is that it breaks down this seemingly elusive concept of success into easy and manageable ways of doing things. It looks at what an individual can and should do, focusing more on their self, bringing a feeling of control in a situation which does not always make one feel like one is in charge. Savita and Bharat have created a masterpiece through simplifying concepts, making them easy to imbibe and internalize while highlighting the role of the internal self of the individual and not just the extraneous situations and elements that contribute to success. This is a must read for all young people who look to climb the ladder of success.

—Dr Samir Parikh MD, Psychiatrist, Director Department of Mental Health, Fortis Healthcare

For those seeking a short 'capsule course' on how to succeed in life, this simple, straightforward and highly engaging book by the Wakhlus is the perfect answer. Using attention-grabbing stories and a reader-friendly writing style, they highlight the key skills needed for succeeding in life—and illustrate the steps by which to develop them. Readers will surely find going through this book—especially the practical tips in it—a greatly rewarding experience.

—Dr J. Singh, Professor of Organizational Behavior, and Chairman International Relations, XLRI

In their very insightful book, Bharat and Savita use anecdotes and cases that are sure to provide young professionals lessons necessary for being not only successful but also happy. By offering easy to use strategies for getting rid of hard-wired beliefs and attitudes they make it possible for readers to become aware of their inner self, which is essential for dealing with the complexities of their work or personal life. This book is a must read for all those keen to enrich their lives by simplifying it.

—*Madhu Chawla, Founder and Director, Madhu Chawla*
Design Trend Private Ltd

I just finished reading your book *Navigating the Maze*. It is a wonderful, well written book and indeed, offers simple and smarter strategies to fast-track success. This book is unarguably an excellent investment which eloquently decodes and unravels the essentials in modern man's quest of a fulfilling and meaningful life. It is no exaggeration to say that both of you together have done a flawless job with your enthusiasm, dedication and eloquence. The stories and anecdotes make it a collector's item for the young and old alike. I personally enjoyed reading your book and have also benefited from it because it gave me an opportunity to reflect and introspect about my own life, relationships and personal goals.

A good addition to my personal collection!

—*Vijayam Kartha, Educational Consultant*

The Handbook of Holistic Tonic for the Modern Day Manager could perhaps be an alternative name for this book, and every career person, young or old, should have one.

And should read it at least once every couple of years!

Down to earth and yet profound, Savita and Bharat take the reader along an elaborate journey spanning consciousness, self-worth, attitude, positivity and everything else to do with interiority; and then guide us down the path of relationships, teamwork, intention, empathy, communication, compassion and everything... yes everything...else to do with EQ and interactive excellence. Weaving all this into that intricate tapestry called life, and relating it to leadership and quality in the workplace is the book's signal achievement.

Easy to read, and with lots of anecdotes and allegories, you will certainly enjoy this book. And read it more than once.

—*Jehangir Ardeshir, Group CEO and Director Supervisory*
Board at Forbes Marshal

NAVIGATING
the
MAZE

NAVIGATING
the
MAZE

Simple, Smarter Strategies
to Fast-track Success

BHARAT WAKHLU
SAVITA BHAN WAKHLU

Los Angeles | London | New Delhi
Singapore | Washington DC | Melbourne

First published in 2017 by

SAGE Publications India Pvt Ltd
B1/I-1 Mohan Cooperative Industrial Area
Mathura Road, New Delhi 110 044, India
www.sagepub.in

SAGE Publications Inc
2455 Teller Road
Thousand Oaks, California 91320, USA

SAGE Publications Ltd
1 Oliver's Yard, 55 City Road
London EC1Y 1SP, United Kingdom

SAGE Publications Asia-Pacific Pte Ltd
3 Church Street
#10-04 Samsung Hub
Singapore 049483

Published by Vivek Mehra for SAGE Publications India Pvt Ltd, typeset in 11/13 pt Adobe Caslon by Fidus Design Pvt. Ltd., Chandigarh 31D and printed at Sai Print-o-Pack, New Delhi..

Library of Congress Cataloging-in-Publication Data Available

ISBN: 978-93-860-4237-8 (PB)

SAGE Team: Sachin Sharma, Priya Arora, Apeksha Sharma and Rajinder Kaur

*To all our teachers, gurus and spiritual masters
who manifest at different stages in our lives
and helped us navigate our passage.*

Bulk Sales

SAGE India offers special discounts
for purchase of books in bulk.
We also make available special imprints
and excerpts from our books on demand.

For orders and enquiries, write to us at

Marketing Department
SAGE Publications India Pvt Ltd
B1/I-1, Mohan Cooperative Industrial Area
Mathura Road, Post Bag 7
New Delhi 110044, India

E-mail us at **marketing@sagepub.in**

Get to know more about SAGE

Be invited to SAGE events, get on our mailing list.
Write today to **marketing@sagepub.in**

This book is also available as an e-book.

Contents

Foreword

In the quagmire of everyday existence, we are bound to come across occasionally difficult situations when, with all our education and experience, we feel like lost and getting drowned in the vortex of an ocean. This is particularly so with young professionals who find it embarrassing and delicate to discuss their problems with their colleagues, friends or even parents. How do they then navigate themselves to a safe shore?

Wakhlus' book *Navigating the Maze—Simple, Smarter Strategies to Fast-track Success* provides the answer and comfort to the young professionals facing the above-mentioned situations.

The authors have advocated that our unseen but enormous powers of 'mind and intelligence' should be harnessed as a ferry and boatman for this purpose. The authors must have taken inspiration from *Sloka* (stanza) 5 of Chapter 6 of the Bhagavad Gita for drawing the contours of their book. The sloka exhorts, 'One should lift oneself by one's own efforts; and should not despise oneself; for one's own self is one's own friend; and one's own self is one's own enemy.' Our own inner faculties of mind and intelligence—only human beings are endowed with such faculties—determine our response, outlook and judgements in any situation. These sentient senses determine the quality of our lives—whether joyful, contented, elevating or sorrowful.

This book is diligently divided into three main chapters that present the basic themes into three categories: (a) self-mastery, (b) interactional excellence and (c) the world of work. Each chapter in turn has a number of sections that cover important elements of the three main issues. In addition, at the end of each chapter there is a section that, along with those in Part II, is intended to provide answers to those frequently asked questions that haunt the young minds. Thus, this book is a complete answer to the troubled minds enabling them to adorn virtues such as characteral excellence, behavioural majesty and interactional elegance.

The authors have prescribed simple but appropriate smart strategies to fast-track success, with the help of anecdotes, short stories and their own recorded observations of fellowmen in dilemma.

This book is written in a simple and effortless style—a distinct style of their own—lucid and compelling to drive home their points to make the subject easy for grasping.

This book fills a long-felt vacuum generally experienced by struggling professionals, whether they are fresh from college or with some experience in middle or senior managerial levels.

I wish to compliment the authors for the way they have handled a difficult theme in a very professional and accomplished manner. I am sure this book will be a well sought after possession by young and enterprising minds.

Dr E. Sreedharan
Principal Adviser,
Delhi Metro Rail Corporation

Preface

Navigating the Maze recognizes that today's generation (the IGen) comprises impatient digital natives, who pride their individuality and doing things 'their way'. This book acknowledges and *appreciates* these traits, and builds up on them. It equips this generation with the self-knowledge and the skills and competencies that help all readers joyfully traverse the challenges and opportunities that they face in a changing world. It also encourages readers to delve into the quiet space within, thereby connecting them with their own interiority and harnessing the vast *inner resources* to their advantage.

In the course of our many interactions with young men and women over the years, we have grasped that youngsters are keen to live their lives in ways that promote health, happiness, love, relationships, joyful work and prosperity. This is the reason that this book focuses on three critical ideas: self-mastery, interpersonal excellence and the world of work. Introducing the right skills and capabilities in these three important areas of life, youngsters are primed for fast-tracking success.

This book has its roots in a project that we worked on in 1997, while we were in Jamshedpur (Bharat worked for Tata Steel then). At that time we jointly contributed a fortnightly column for *The Telegraph* that was published from Kolkata. This column was called 'What You May Not Have Learnt at Business School' and gave readers in the towns of Eastern India a chance to get insights into the professional, relational and technological issues that they were grappling with. Surprisingly, even 20 years later, many of the same themes remain at the heart of the concerns expressed by young professionals today.

We are confident that if the simple, smarter strategies contained in this book are internalized and put into practice, together they would make a qualitative difference in the lives of people. We have placed emphasis on helping our readers get straight to the essence of what is needed to live a life that is fulfilling and successful. We have also suggested ways of entering the quiet space of our interiority, so that our readers too can plumb into its depths and learn how to live happy, healthy and meaningful lives. This capability is even more in need in this day and age, when messages from advertisers, the noise from sophisticated hucksters promoting ideas or the distractions of a smartphone force us to be in a state of perpetual tension and stress.

The collective influences of an overbearing technology, the constant noise from multiple sources and the pressures on each of us to consume more and more, even as we realize that our planet cannot sustain wanton consumption, have made our lives truly complicated. Getting out of the 'rat race' that such a world might stimulate and returning to our lives of health, happiness, love, prosperity and fulfilment calls for opening up to life, by simplifying our relationship with ourselves and our interiority, as well as with everyone and everything that might touch our lives. In doing so, we begin to *live life* and *open up* to the things that are truly valuable to us and that make for days well-lived.

We suggest that the ideas in this book be imbibed at a time when you, dear reader, are not distracted. We would even suggest that you find some quiet time, when you are not going to be disturbed, to go through this book. That would help you reflect and understand what we are trying to share with you. Remember, we are not giving you answers to the problems that you, or many other people, might be facing. Instead, we are arming you with the skills, the knowledge, the smarts and the strategies that would make your life worthwhile and successful in the manner in which you choose. The essential tools that we share with you herein will help you enjoy—boldly and confidently—whatever life might offer you, while simultaneously helping you enrich your unique journey.

On our part, we have made this book really simple and easy to read. It is peppered with stories and anecdotes that pithily drive home important truths. Throughout we have tried to offer you the essential implements, the tools and the tackle that you would need to navigate the mysterious maze of life. But above all, we point to the source of the wellspring of pure guidance that your interiority offers you for free.

We appreciate that this book has come into your life with a purpose. It is our firm conviction that as you apply what you learn in this book, it will unclutter things around you in ways that are both uncomplicated and playful. The simple, smarter strategies along with the choices you make would then put you on a fast track to receive in abundance, from the majesty and the glory of *life* itself.

Acknowledgements

To begin with, we would like to thank Sachin Sharma, the Commissioning Editor at SAGE. His constant support and gentle prodding to adhere to the tight deadlines is deeply appreciated. His able team comprising Priya Arora, Apeksha Sharma and Rajinder Kaur worked meticulously and collaboratively with us to bring this book into its present form.

We both have been blessed to have had supportive and enlightened families, where our elders planted the seeds for continuous personal growth early in our lives. Significant elders served as positive role models, demonstrating an ethic for life that was underpinned on integrity, service and excellence. We are grateful to all of them.

Our teachers, mentors and gurus have had a major influence in enhancing our learning and development. Guidance has come to us in diverse settings and at different stages of our lives. We are immensely thankful to all those wise and nurturing individuals who supported our respective journeys.

We have been fortunate to have been inspired and introduced to our own infinite, inner resources by our Spiritual Guru, Swami Bhoomananda Tirthaji of Thrissur, Kerala. His loving guidance and precious pointers in our journey are gratefully acknowledged.

Dr E. Sreedharan deserves our special thanks and appreciation for generously devoting time to writing the foreword for this book. As a renowned and successful technocrat and executive, his words reinforce the essential message of this book.

The millennials in our circle of family and friends promptly responded to our specific queries about what needed to be included in this book. Many thanks are due to them for their insights and inputs.

The live, 'real-time' questions that were put to us by students of business schools form an important part of this book. Thank you all for sharing your queries. We hope this compilation serves as your personal lodestar.

Our sincere appreciation and thanks also go to Brother Prasanna Swaroopa, our 'guru-brother', who diligently went through the manuscript and shared valuable feedback for improvement. We are also immensely grateful to all those eminent professionals who provided their written testimonials for this book. Our niece, Nitya too deserves thanks for helping crystallize the cover design for this book.

Finally, a special word of thanks to Raja Bose, of *The Times of India* group, Lucknow. He was instrumental in featuring our column, 'What You May Not Have Learnt at Business School', while he worked with *The Telegraph* in Jamshedpur, many years ago. This book evolved from that initiative.

Getting Ready for the Adventure!

(Using This Book Smartly)

O ur life's journeys are unique. Each of us consciously needs to forge a path that is uniquely ours. Pursuing our *own journey* is the most optimal, productive and joyful way of achieving our full potential and of living a life of abundance, happiness and well-being.

If we calmly reflect on this idea, it makes the whole endeavour of trying to 'be like the others' or 'following the herd' completely unnecessary and inappropriate. The exhortations—from society, elders, peers, advertisers and so many others—to emulate successful men and women are completely unbefitting of the great and wondrous gifts and talents that indwell in each and every one of us.

This also implies that the definition of 'success' will be different for every one of us! There cannot ever be just one concept of success. There will be as many routes and possibilities of success as there are people.

While contemplating the title of this book, we realized that each reader would have to choose *his or her own definition* of success. Thereafter, each one would chart his or her own course to reach that position. For all of us, our unique journey is akin to going through a maze: where we choose to *make our own path* to the goal that we wish to achieve!

In order to fast-track movement on that uniquely chosen path, some essential personal qualities and competencies are vital. These are self-mastery, interactional excellence and an appropriate approach to one's world of work. These very themes comprise the first three chapters in Part I of this book.

So what might be a smart way of using this book?

We suggest that you start with Chapter 1 and proceed sequentially with Chapter 2 and then Chapter 3. You are free to flit between sections within a chapter, but we strongly suggest that you should move on to the next chapter only after you have gone through each of the sections in the preceding chapter.

This is essential since many ideas that you will encounter in the subsequent chapters would be introduced in the previous one. It would also be appropriate to re-read any section (or a part of it) that you think needs to be refreshed. This also applies to the questions at the end of each chapter. The responses to the questions in this book are based on our collective experience of what the most appropriate ways are to deal with the stated issue. It is worthwhile to mention, however, that some questions pertain to fairly complex situations (such as the act of firing an employee) and while we may have given broad guidance in our responses, many such issues need to be *carefully* weighed and acted upon on the basis of the actual context, the cultural aspects, the facts of the situation as well as a desire to avoid any unintended consequences.

Part II of this book consists of questions germane to the theme of this book. They cover secondary but significant facets of personal performance and effectiveness. 'Making Impactful Presentations', 'Social and Business Etiquette' and 'Cross-cultural Effectiveness' together comprise Chapter 4.

All the questions included in this book are real-time and current and have been asked of us by young professionals.

Internalizing the high points of our responses to these queries is a beginning. But then modifying and refining your response and behaviour in similar situations will depend upon your own 'understanding' and a 'diagnosis' of the circumstances.

Let the Adventure begin!

PART I

The Essential Overview

1

Self-mastery

(A) Thinking, Feeling and Behaving

The Inner World of Feelings and Emotions

We were flying from New York to New Delhi on this long, non-stop flight. We usually watch a couple of movies between sleep and doing some reading, so on this flight we watched a relatively new animation film *Inside Out*. Both of us just loved it! That was the 'feeling' we experienced.

If you have not seen this very simple, but elegant, story of a little girl called Riley and the five emotions—anger, disgust, fear, sadness and joy—that make the other animated characters in the movie, we suggest you do so without delay. It is a simple story but gives a wonderful glimpse into the working of our minds. Riley's story demonstrates how our emotions affect the way we perceive the world, how we relate with others and how even our past experiences are coloured by the emotions we associate with those events!

Feelings and emotions make us human. Though the terms 'feelings' and 'emotions' are used interchangeably in popular literature, there is a subtle difference.

Emotions are sudden, short-term *reactions* to stimuli that we encounter in our interactions with the outside world. Biologically, and through the process of evolution, emotions have helped humans survive and protect themselves against dangers. But emotions also give life colour, texture and richness, and add meaning to the experiences that we have in the course of our many interactions.

Imagine a primitive, *near-human* hunter-gatherer (a Neanderthal man, for instance) around 50,000 years ago wandering with a few other men of his kind in a dense forest. If anyone of the persons in the group were to notice (or see) a sabre-toothed tiger (Smilodon), that would constitute a sensory stimulus. Based on the prior experiences of these hunters and their thinking patterns related to past encounters with a ferocious Smilodon or any other wild beast, they would experience emotion.

If anyone of them had thereby acquired insights into the behaviour of such an animal and also learnt what might occur if the beast were to attack, then that hunter would experience either fear or aggression and his body's endocrine system would swiftly bring about bodily changes to aid survival.

Biochemicals flowing into the bloodstream would enhance the body's functional parameters, preparing the hunter to either hunt the beast forcefully (the *fight* response) or to ensure self-preservation by running away (the *flight* response). In either situation, the hunter would experience rapid breathing, a racy pulse and raised blood pressure.

Feelings are the *collective memory* of emotions that have been experienced. When a child experiences positive emotions, such as 'joy' or 'enthusiasm' in the presence of his or her parents and extended family, the child's brain is likely to be 'hard-wired' to experience feelings of 'love' and 'contentment' whenever in the presence of family. Obviously, as the movie *Inside Out* also depicts, our world view is determined on the basis of our feelings towards people, animals, events and places, because we experience emotions whenever we encounter stimuli.

In ancient India, the power of emotions was recognized and accepted as an integral part of the human experience. Emotions in Sanskrit are called *bhāvas*, and many scholars like sage Bharatā—who wrote the treatise on performing arts called *NātyaShāstra*—presented details of the manner in which actors can evoke certain emotions in the audience through the interplay of eight predominant themes (*rasas*).

Emotions Affect Behaviour

Think of the times when you were a child: say about five or six years of age. Which things or events frightened you then? How do you *feel*—at this time—when you think about those events?

You would agree that as children even 'normal', non-threatening stimuli can evoke feelings of fear. A rope lying in a dark corner of the garden may look like a snake. A pet kitten with sharp claws or a prancing puppy that bites can evoke a lifelong fear of cats or dogs.

Coming back to the thought experiment: How did you feel when you remembered childhood experiences? Were any emotions evoked in this moment?

Even as human adults, our feelings—which reside in our minds, intertwined with memories—can give rise to the very same emotions that we first experienced! This is true for positive as well as negative emotions. Even when we may realize through our intellect that the negative feelings (of fear or anxiety, for instance) are unfounded and misplaced, still it takes a little while for the emotions to settle.

A young girl child accidentally falls into a swimming pool. Though rescued and saved from drowning in time, the experience of being underwater, breathless and taking some water into her tiny lungs leaves the little girl fearful of water bodies. While growing up she makes no attempt to overcome this fear, nor is she helped by her family to tide over the fear of water bodies. She never learns to swim. She is also very reluctant to go to the beach or for picnics by the lake.

This young woman is invited by friends for a boat ride in a nearby reservoir. The very thought of being in a boat evokes her feelings of fear once again. Her fearful experiences of childhood 'fast-forward' into the present! The woman breaks into a cold sweat while her pulse rises and she feels limp in her legs. She might actually *feel* quite sick and make that an excuse for not agreeing to go.

At the level of her intellect she probably 'knows' that this visceral fear is unfounded. But she does not know how to overcome it.

We all have deep-seated and habituated patterns of thinking that cause us to react automatically to certain stimuli. In the case of the young woman, it was just the thought of being in water that triggered her mind to react with the same emotions that she had experienced as a child.

Attitudes and Beliefs

Early one morning, the CEO of an organization placed a notice on the main notice board at the office entrance that said: 'The person, who was blocking your growth in this organization, has passed away. A prayer meeting for the dear departed will be held in the canteen at 11 am.'

Everyone felt sad that a colleague had moved on. No one knew who it was; however, as the day wore on, curiosity got the better of all and everyone assembled in the large canteen. Here they saw a shiny coffin, with its lid open, at the other end. The entire canteen was so full that there were people standing in the hallway trying to be a part of the proceedings.

The CEO thanked everyone for their presence, but still did not reveal the name of the colleague. Instead, he invited the assembled employees to make a single file and go past the coffin, as a mark of respect, and to see for themselves who had passed on.

As the line progressed, all the employees who glanced into the coffin, without exception, wore a shocked look on their faces. Nobody uttered a word. They were completely dumbfounded.

Within the coffin was a large mirror. When the employees peered in, they saw their own faces! None of them could imagine that the CEO was using the occasion and the drama to share a powerful message: 'You are the person blocking your potential!'

Nobody can imagine that we ourselves—and our automatic patterns of thinking—can become the biggest blocks to our individual growth!

Our automatic thinking patterns form our 'attitudes' and 'beliefs'. The interplay of our attitudes and beliefs, on interactional or other stimuli, yield a range of emotions.

An attitude is our *judgemental evaluation* of an 'attitude object' (which could be anything, really!). In the anecdote above, most people held this view that it was someone *outside* who was blocking their growth. The CEO shook his employees into questioning this assumption, through a contrived event.

Beliefs are built on attitudes and help create a pattern in a person's mind that makes something seem true, even in the *absence* of evidence which could confirm that belief. Even an *arbitrary* attitudinal evaluation begins to ring true.

Here is an example: A child in junior school is bullied by a few boys from a rival school, wearing their uniform of white shirts and green trousers. The young child associates the experience with the uniform and forms a belief that *anyone* wearing the colours white and green is a bully. Even after a few years when this (by now) older boy encounters a courteous and decent scholar wearing the same uniform, he is unable to interact with him freely because his belief—that all boys from the rival school are bullies—is resurrecting the emotion of fear in him!

It is clear that if we *assume* that whatever our mind tells us is true, we can be in a place where going through life as it is can be emotionally painful. Furthermore, if we do not question our beliefs—and ascertain if these are based on rational reasoning—we will live our lives being completely limited by the emotions that we experienced as children.

There are countless people in this world whose normal lives are greatly impaired by irrational fears of such things as flying, spiders, pets or whatever else may have impacted their minds when they were impressionable.

Assumptions Are a Minefield!

Have you ever looked at how the word ASSUME is spelt? ASS U ME!

Yes, if you assume something, you make an ass (the animal!) of yourself and the others who are affected!

Assumptions are an automatic thinking pattern. They are often based on a deep-seated, internally articulated notion that 'I know everything.' There is a pansophical delusion in people who assume that they can read the minds of others; or know what the *real* reason for an event or another's statement is. And who think that they can correctly infer why something is happening in a certain way!

Obviously, such a broad and sweeping attitude can give rise to assumptions that can be completely out of whack with the reality of many a situation!

This intrapersonal thinking pattern can affect interpersonal communication in a significant manner by becoming a serious barrier to relating with others (more about this in Section 'Communicating Assertively' of Chapter 2). Unfortunately, if a person sees the breakdown of communication as a 'problem with others' rather than questioning one's own attitudes, beliefs and assumptions, it can only make matters more complex and difficult.

As with other automatic thoughts, there is a need to question one's assumptions at every point in any sort of interaction. Even when you are quietly ruminating by yourself, what you think about someone can actually colour the manner in which you'll interact with that person when you actually encounter him or her! Your mind will be running over the same script—the assumptions and the judgements—that you have internalized, when you were just thinking about her!

What is not so well known is that all of us have a self-generated dialogue going on in our minds. In fact, many psychologists equate thinking with speaking to oneself. This thinking-driven, inner dialogue is known as 'self-talk'. When you think, notice how you speak with yourself.

The manner in which you speak with yourself in your head—whether angrily or in someone else's voice—also determines if it is 'you' who is thinking on your own or whether you are simply playing back what you have picked up from books, elders or other people in your life; and whose voices you are automatically mimicking in your thoughts!

Many believe that self-talk is a *form* of thinking that is beyond our control. This view is not true. Like all thoughts or beliefs, self-talk too can be observed with awareness. One can actually observe the welling up of ideas and the commencement of an inner dialogue. The dialogue within can be triggered off by a stimulus from the outside, or the *mere recall* of a past event or conversation. Self-talk that is actually affecting our lives and relationships in negative ways would need to be modified.

Why would our self-talk affect our lives? The reason: Self-talk serves as the substrate upon which assumptions are formed. If we allow inappropriate self-talk to colour our reality, then engaging with others can be adversely affected. Even our behaviour is influenced by our self-talk and the assumptions, attitudes and beliefs that such internal dialogue reinforces.

Expectations Are Also Assumptions

A man in Japan was rowing his boat on the lake one dark, wintry evening. His lantern too was low on oil, so he was eager to get to the shore swiftly. As he was moving along, he noticed the faint silhouette of another boat coming in his direction. Concerned that the two boats might collide, he shouted a warning to the other boatman. Yet, that boat seemed to be moving directly towards him.

'Hey, get back! We don't want to damage our boats, back off man!' he shouted angrily. Still the boat stayed on course and was by now close enough for him to stand up and angrily use his oar to hit—what he *thought* was—the other boatman! 'Take that, you fool!' the man shouted as he brought his oar to hit the other boatman in the darkness. The oar made a loud thud but it just hit the side of the other boat.

Then it dawned on him! The other boat was empty. There was nobody in it. It had been drifting on the water. His rage was a creation of his own mind! He *expected* the other boat to have a boatman too and was, therefore, directing all his anger towards him.

Wise people—men and women from many diverse cultures—have, through the ages, emphasized that one of the secret ingredients for going through life with the minimum amount of emotional buffeting is to work with the least *expectations* from any situation.

Expectations are an *assumed response pattern* to a situation, 'based on what we consider important to us'. In the above-narrated story, the man expected the other boat to be manned by a responsible boatman. The empty boat, therefore, caused anger to well up in his mind.

If you are a person who loves gifts, and you give a close friend a birthday gift that is thoughtfully chosen and pricey, you may assume—rightly or wrongly is not in question right now—that you too would get as valuable a gift from this friend on your birthday. This is an expectation.

You assume a pattern in your mind and then place a high value on that pattern unfurling (in reality). Your temperament places significance on the expectation.

So if the expectation is met, you stand 'vindicated' in that your assumptions have turned out the way you wanted and you are, therefore, 'happy'. Interestingly, the expectations you make can be on anything that you consider important. They can concern a situation or an event. The way one's supervisor speaks to one, for example, or the manner in which your organization rewards your hard work. Or it might be about the value of the gift that your elder brothers or sisters present you on your wedding day or even the kind of car that is sent to receive you at the airport when you arrive in a different city on a business trip.

There are two fundamental issues here that we all need to know. First, expectations are based on *our own perceptions* of what we think is valuable, appropriate or essential for us. The corresponding assumptions and self-talk emanate from this state of mind.

It is in the very fabric of life, and of human existence itself, that all of a person's expectations cannot be met! There will be unplanned events that can arise or occur, despite the best intentions of all the parties concerned, throwing even the best laid plans into a tizzy! This implies that by forming expectations, in the first place, we are setting ourselves up for disappointments.

The second point relates to the fact that expectations that we form in our minds are known only to us. Others cannot read our minds, and therefore, they cannot meet our expectations precisely, 'unless we communicate what we expect them to do for us'! The assumption that all those you are close to, or intimate with, have the gift of *mind-reading* and are, therefore, fully conversant with your nuanced expectations is another foolish assumption that causes great pain in relationships. The truth is that unless we communicate to others what is important to us, and share unambiguously with them our expectations, there is no way that one's expectations will be met.

Many people when questioned as to why they did not communicate with their friend/loved one what they wanted from them usually respond by saying:

'They should have known, because they are close to me!'

Even those we are close to cannot read our minds!
So sharing our desires and expectations with others is good. Otherwise, expectations like assumptions are a treacherous minefield too!

Responding, Rather than Reacting to Stimuli

The natural state of rest for our brains is manifest when we are calm, content and neither fearful nor desiring something avidly. This is the state when we are able to exercise *right choices*.

Breaking the barriers of self-limiting beliefs or erroneous assumptions and exercising right choices is a critical aspect of becoming an effective person. If we choose not to question what beliefs we hold and how we think, we can live our entire lives completely enslaved by flawed patterns in our minds. Sufi mystics in the Orient encourage their students to examine the assumptions behind their actions and then examine the assumptions behind the assumptions. We all need to do that too.

Prejudices, too, have their source in beliefs that individuals and communities harbour and which get continually reinforced. Unless one questions and disputes the basis of these beliefs and works to dump them, the underlying evaluations and attitudes keep on emerging and colouring our responses to stimuli. Much like computer programs that have bugs in the software but which run nonetheless once given the command.

So what we feel is, indeed, based on the thinking patterns of our mind. But whether we would let an 'erroneous belief' hijack our emotions and force us to *react* to a stimulus, rather than *respond* to it, is a *choice* that we all have. In fact, Dr Daniel Goleman refers to overwhelming and sudden emotional reactions in certain people as being an 'amygdala hijack' caused by a very ordinary stimulus. The amygdala is a small gland inside our brains that has played, and continues to play, a role in our survival as a species, because it forces us to fight or avoid things that threaten us.

The process of responding requires us to deliberately bring our minds into a state of calm *awareness*, where we can reflect on all the inputs and choose a response. Remember, reacting is an *instinctive* response, based on a primitive part of our brains.

It becomes relatively easy to initiate the process of changing hardened, self-limiting beliefs if we work with awareness. Systematically identifying, and then gradually eliminating, beliefs that are irrational, challenging, flawed or otherwise erroneous may be a long-drawn process, but it brings benefits. A primary benefit is: we are liberated from the habits of our conditioned past and the prisons of habitual thinking.

Our Brains: An Evolutionary Three-in-one

The modern human brain is an amazing organ, comprising billions of neurons. Evolution favoured the addition of more advanced functionalities to the original structures found in lower animals. Thus, we notice that the modern human brain has three main parts.

The original reptilian brain—comprising the brain stem and the cerebellum, is the oldest of the three brain parts. The reptilian brain within the whole human brain controls the body's vital functions such as our heart's performance, lung function and breathing, body temperature as well as balance and stability. The reptilian brain was hard-wired to ensure the survival of that species, by controlling basic responses to stimuli in an automatic, instinctive and instantaneous fashion. The reptilian brain obviously did a splendid job of ensuring survival to enable basic reptilian animal life to have survived and to have evolved to a point where humans—first as *Homo erectus* and then *Homo sapiens*—came into being.

The second part of the brain is the 'limbic' brain. It lies in between the reptilian brain and the neocortex (the third and the most modern part of our brains, also known as the iso-cortex) and hence has this name (derived from the Latin word meaning 'on the edge'). The first mammals on earth (that appeared about 200 million years ago) had a brain that incorporated the reptilian and the limbic brains.

Predatory mammals had a more developed limbic component than the herbivores because this part of the brain is a storehouse of past experiences and the underlying 'likeable' or 'disgusting' emotions felt. That would have been an important piece of information for a mammal involved in the more difficult task of catching prey than those that were simply grazers.

This part of the brain—which includes vital structures such as the hippocampus and the amygdala—together with the hypothalamus forms the seat where unconscious value judgements and evaluations are made by us. Naturally, whatever is stored in this part of our brains has a bearing on the way we interact with the outside world as well as other people. It's worthwhile to note that the hip-pocampus, the amygdala and the hypothalamus are fully developed at birth in a human baby, unlike the third part of the brain—the neocortex.

The third part of our brains comprises the neocortex, which are the two large lobes that enclose the limbic brain. This part of our brains started to develop in the early primates about 3 million years ago and has contributed substantially to the expansion of the capabilities related to language, music, abstract thought, consciousness, imagination, creativity and learning. This is the part that is truly 'plastic' and exhibits what neurosurgeons call *neuroplasticity*: the capability and the unlimited potential to learn new things and unlearn the old. However, this part of our brains develops its neurological capacity only gradually.

An important aspect that relates to how we deal with stimuli has to do with the fact that the three different parts of our brain have a number of neural connections that enable the brain to function as a single organ. However, because of evolutionary reasons the pathways between the reptilian, limbic brain and the neocortex are not uniform. There are many more pathways, for instance, leading from the limbic brain to the neocortex than there are in the reverse direction. This is significant and has a bearing on why we sometimes experience very little time between a stimulus and our emotional and behavioural reaction to it.

So when a stimulus occurs, there are two ways for this information to reach the limbic brain. The short, imprecise but direct route from the hypothalamus to the amygdala is one route. The other is the long, slow and *precise* route from the neocortex. The information reaches the amygdala quickly, because—in evolution's creative way—it was apparent that in the face of real danger, even a few fractions of a second can make the difference between survival and death of the animal.

Based on the stimulus and on account of past memories of danger or a risk that can affect survival, the limbic brain will send a signal that can stimulate the sympathetic nervous system to react immediately, preparing the organism for a response that will assure survival. Thus, a human's heartbeat can rise and the body would be primed to fight or run to safety. Different emotional responses could also arise.

However, after this initial reaction, if the neocortex—with its powers of discrimination and judgement in conjunction with the hippocampus—were to realize that the stimulus is not dangerous after all, then the limbic brain will receive a message a few seconds later and be directed to 'cool off'. The body and the emotions would come back to normal, once again, and the human would have only experienced a momentary scare.

So, our brains really are three organs in one!

Why Your Best Friend Flipped!

Many of us have had this experience: Our best friends, people whom we respect and trust, suddenly fly into a rage at something that we said to them. Something really innocuous and trivial (according to us) seems to have pushed their hot buttons and now we do not speak to one another anymore.

Does this sound familiar? It is far more common than one would like to believe. Obviously somewhere in the minds of our friends, they must have assigned an 'unpleasant' or 'dangerous' label to our stimuli (the ideas that we shared and the words we used) and their limbic brains quickly set off a survival signal and made them ready to fight!

There is thankfully a way out of the overarching control that our limbic brains exercise on us. We *can* create new pathways from our neocortex to the limbic brain. Thereby, sudden reactions can be tempered with richer and timely information from the discriminating part of our brains and help us to respond—rather than react uncontrollably—to stimuli.

Since neurons that fire together wire together, the more we respond with awareness, the more we diminish the relevance of the instinctive neural pathways that force us to react.

Pavlov's Dogs

Ivan Pavlov was a Russian scientist who died in 1936. As he was studying mammals and how their digestion worked, he realized that the dogs that he was working on would salivate and drool even when someone in a white lab coat would pass by their kennels and not just when food was offered. He dug deeper into this phenomenon and realized that the dogs had *learnt* to associate the white lab coats with the arrival of food and hence would drool in anticipation.

Pavlov demonstrated with even more refined experiments, thereafter, that the mere association of the ringing of a bell with the arrival of food was enough to make the dogs salivate even when the bell was rung alone. He called this process classical conditioning.

Humans too learn to deal with their environments by interpreting stimuli and forming connections based on how they feel, thereby understanding new experiences. Since humans also grow with other people, the positive encouragements or negative punishments they receive as they *interpret* the environmental stimuli also help in the creation of their beliefs and attitudes. That is why no two personalities are ever identical.

However, unlike animals, we humans possess a beautiful quality in our wakeful, alert states of mind: namely, the ability to *think rationally* and *make conscious choices*. These are a key capability set of the neocortex and along with the right kind of learning it gives us the capacity to be creative, happy and socially effective problem solvers.

Our critical thinking abilities are obviously impacted by the diversity and the quantum of the inputs—the experiences, the rules, values, beliefs and ideas—that we receive or form from our social interactions and the environment in which we grow up and operate. When we are young we tend to internalize—often without questioning—many of these ideas and beliefs and 'carry' them with us into adulthood. Such cognitive baggage—or the remnants of all our past emotional responses to stimuli and the subjective value judgements placed on them—is collectively termed 'conditioning'.

There is a way to trump the connections in the brain that have been formed through thousands of years of evolution. Besides, as we have shared earlier, the brain's plasticity and ability to grow for long years after the human has reached adulthood gives us the power to question our assumptions and beliefs and much of the conditioning that resides in our brains. The questioning and disputing of our conditioning and the learnt 'conditioned responses' enables us to 'respond smartly' and 'not react abruptly' to stimuli.

We have the power within us to behave far more 'elegantly' than Pavlov's dogs!

Evolving to the Higher You

No two human beings are the same. Just as no two snowflakes or the seeds of the same plant are ever alike, even people are unique in every possible way. There can never be another you, ever, in the whole cosmos.

This is a good time to mull on this idea. Take a pen and write the following statement:

'I am unique, and there is one, and only one ___ (add your name here) with my special gifts and talents in the whole Universe!'

At this point in time you are 'whole' and 'complete', not deficient or imperfect. You are at that stage in your life's journey where you have all the knowledge and skills that you need to be where you are.

To reach your full potential, however, you may choose to do some regular 'spring cleaning' in your life because what was useful for your life's journey till now may now have to be dropped. Once you've crossed a river, it would be silly to carry the boat on your back!

So jettisoning erroneous patterns of thinking and unlearning our conditioned beliefs are an essential part of evolving to your higher selves. This process calls for patience and considerable practice. Sometimes, we might even experience emotional anguish and guilt as we throw away what is no longer useful to us.

The feelings of guilt come from deciding to dump what we may have taken from others a long time back and then treated as the unassailable truth. The mind associates the dumping of those ideas with the dumping of the persons from whom you had obtained those ideas.

If not the guilt, then it is the despair that emanates from the awareness that your whole personality, identity and life till the moment of discernment were built on flawed assumptions and beliefs that have no resemblance with the truth.

What you had thought was a poisonous snake turned out to be a rope after all! With it comes the realization that you have had fiery arguments and broken friendships based on such a glaring falsehood. It is indeed a painful realization. The emotions of guilt, anger and the pain one experiences in such situations is real. These feelings are aggravated as we then think of ways to make amends: Do we have the courage to own up and apologize? Or should we continue with the charade and pretend that nothing has changed? These are tough decisions.

In small doses, feeling a little guilt can be healthy and serves as a guide for appropriate behaviour. It can be useful to regulate actions that are harmful to us, such as extreme overeating, smoking pot or getting high on drugs.

But if guilt is felt as we question and attempt to dispute some of the erroneous patterns in our minds, then we need to be watchful. As has been shared earlier, this irrational or unhealthy guilt emanates from a level where we associate the beliefs we are questioning with people whom we love.

The flawed logic that causes guilt and hurt prompts us to believe that since we are dumping the conditioning associated with people we love, we are disowning them! This is obviously not true.

Admonishments that lurk in the mind as 'must' or 'should' or 'should never' and the like, can be a source of guilt because as a child any violation was associated with a parental reprimand or punishment. Now, even as adults, we each have a part of us playing that role of a punitive parent!

So, questioning our self-limiting beliefs and disputing errone-ous conditioning is how we can evolve to our higher selves. If errors are made in the course of being human, we need to accept them and the consequences they may have and move on. Over time, unhealthy guilt and pain—from any source—will diminish if we approach it rationally.

Your own inner 'parent'—who might speak in your thoughts, admonishingly—will be happy to see you coming closer to your full potential by disputing limiting beliefs. Once you appreciate this, you may not feel guilty the next time you pick up another erroneous belief to question and then to dump.

Erroneous Beliefs Trigger Painful Emotions

Choosing thoughts that make you feel good is up to you. Nobody else but you is responsible for how your mind works for you.

If you wish to feel good about life and the relationships that you are in, you can exercise the right choices to deal appropriately with the myriad inputs that you receive from others. Once you calmly reflect on these inputs, and choose your considered response, your behaviour will be more nuanced, appropriate and beneficial.

The Buddha often used stories and parables to explain his experiences to those who came to him with concerns.

One day a rich merchant from a neighbouring kingdom came to the Buddha. He had brought with himself a basketful of delicious mangoes as an offering to the great master. He had come to the Buddha because he was deeply anguished by the fact that his own wife had swindled him of his wealth and had then run away with a younger man.

After the man had conveyed the cause of his sadness and anger, the Buddha asked the man: 'What do you do with mangoes that are rotten?'

'We throw them away, Master,' the merchant replied.

'Now, if you were to keep mangoes in the saddlebag of your horse and not throw out the rotten ones from time to time, what would you say to that?'

'That would be quite foolish, Master. Even the good mangoes would rapidly go bad. Why would anyone do this?'

'The same applies to our thoughts. If we do not throw out our rotten thoughts—thoughts of revenge, anger or hatred for another—we are no different from the foolish man who refuses to throw out the rotten mangoes from his tote. Our lives too can be affected by the negative thoughts that we cling to.'

How would we know which of our beliefs are self-limiting and causing us pain?

This process of self-diagnosis would obviously start with any situation where you find yourself getting angry, feeling hurt or experiencing sadness or anger. If you are miserable on account of something that someone said to you and you find that the conversation is adversely affecting how you feel about your relationship with that person, then that interaction too would be an ideal starting point for some reflection and identifying limiting beliefs.

The rich merchant, too, was experiencing similar feelings and that was why he went to see the Buddha.

There are many ways to 'deal' with erroneous assumptions, or limiting beliefs. In the story, the Buddha suggests to the merchant that he should dump any ideas that are 'rotten' and which do not contribute to his well-being and harmonious relations. This is the most powerful method of all because you can unburden yourself once and for all.

However, this is not always possible to begin with. That is why it also helps to question and thereby dispute one's erroneous beliefs.

When Beliefs Meet Reality

An elderly man 'believes' very strongly that women should not work outside their homes. This man's youngest son decides to get married to a woman who has a job that requires her to travel out of town for a few days every month.

Here is a situation where the older man's beliefs are confronting a new and potentially conflicting state. There are two ways in which this situation can unfurl.

Situation one: If the man 'sticks to his beliefs' (as many might do, since change requires effort) and the son disregards his father's suggestions that his daughter-in-law would not work or travel at all, the man is bound to experience a range of negative emotions. He could 'feel' angry, hurt, humiliated, abandoned or a combination of these emotions. His behaviour would reflect his feelings. Accordingly, the father would start to speak harshly with his son. He would be unable to interact with his daughter-in-law joyfully. He might choose to leave the house and stay somewhere else.

Situation two: The old man is wise and understands that the world has changed, as have gender roles. He 'disputes' and 'dumps' his long-held belief about women working. He feels comfortable that his daughter-in-law needs to travel as part of her work responsibilities. He appreciates that his daughter-in-law has many wonderful qualities and is kind and considerate to him.

What the man feels in either situation is entirely his responsibility and is based on the beliefs that he holds. If the man were unwilling to question and dump his limiting beliefs, he would forever have to experience the consequences of his choice.

In another example, a person harbours two predominant beliefs about 'success' and 'unscrupulous people'. Typically, such beliefs are articulated and reinforced (or disputed) in the self-talk, which makes the 'chatter of thinking' in one's head.

The first belief, when articulated, might read:

'To succeed and be famous, one has to be unscrupulous.'

The second could be:

'I can't stand unscrupulous people.'

Now when such a person meets someone who might be considered 'successful' and 'famous', the person is bound to have difficulties interacting with him or her. Because the two strong beliefs, together, would inevitably cause the person to experience feelings that would force him or her to shy away from anyone he or she perceives as being well known or successful.

The process of discovering what limits a person's behaviour, or a person's effectiveness, in normal situations, is a lifelong process. Once we know what is holding us back, it becomes so much easier to work on those aspects in our thinking. It may take time to deal with or dump such beliefs, but well begun is half-done.

Disputing and Dumping Irrational Beliefs

Events are neutral. How an event affects us, is a factor of how the event 'stimulates' any of our beliefs.

Let us write this down mathematically.

If A is an 'activating event', B represents the 'stimulated belief' in our minds and C represents the 'resultant emotions', then:

$$A \neq C$$

Instead,

$$A * B = C$$

This means that the interaction (represented with the symbol *) of the event *with* our own beliefs, creates the resultant emotions.

You would agree that changing one's beliefs B, so that we feel good in any circumstance is an essential cognitive process. In the long run, it helps us lead a life of equanimity and long-term wellness and harmony.

Disputing and dumping assumptions and beliefs that 'hold us back' need to be done in a rigorous and systematic way. The endeavour is to clear our minds, permanently, of flawed and growth-limiting ideas. Only then would any kind of stimulus A enable us to respond (rather than react) and be calm, steady and collected.

We suggest the following four-step method to dispute our beliefs:

1. 'Identify, and then target for remedying', two or three of the 'core beliefs' or assumptions about a particular situation that are causing us the most emotional pain and discomfort. Identifying the core beliefs is a lot like investigating a crime: we look for evidence of the deeper reasons and the irrational choices we make and determine the cognitive inferences behind why we do, or do not do, something.

   In matters of cognition, the only tools we need are an open, questioning mind and a pen and a sheet of paper to help the process. Often, many irrational core beliefs come in bundles and all the aspects would need to be disputed for lasting ease.

   For instance, if a person experiences stage fright, the fear of being on stage is a symptom of some erroneous set of belief or beliefs; it is not the underlying core belief, though. It helps, therefore, to probe a little deeper by asking further, 'Why am I feeling fearful and anxious, each time I stand on stage in front of an audience?'

   The self-talk 'answer' to such a query would need to be written down.

   For the person in our example it was:

   'I'm concerned that others will laugh at me.'

   A quick analysis of this statement reveals that even this need not be the deeper, core belief and the target that needs to be worked upon and disputed. Further questioning, and asking 'Why? Why?' over and over again, might divulge that the audience's laughter poses a problem, because the person is equating their (occasional) laughter with their (assumed !) derision for that person. The person believes that if anyone in the audience laughs, they are ridiculing and mocking that individual.

Now, this is a clear example of an irrational connection that is being formed between two unconnected events (the audience laughing and the speaker being mocked) that can be severely limiting. Such a belief would be an appropriate one to single out for further work and its eventual jettisoning.

2. Next, one needs to 'broadly determine why the core belief is a source of anxiety or nervousness'. In the case of the speaker with stage fright it has been identified that the person with stage fright 'believes' that anytime a member of the audience laughs, the 'real' intention is to mock the speaker/performer.

This perspective is 'assumed' to be true by the 'downed' persons, based on their past experiences, the memories they hold of such experiences in emotional terms, their temperament and the way they have been brought up.

We all make the error of playing a fortune teller and assuming that we 'know' everything that goes on in another's mind. This can be severely limiting. Irrational thinking patterns such as the one cited earlier can have very real and tangible negative outcomes. So, the essence of the 'irrational assumption behind the belief' has to be identified for it to be disputed appropriately.

3. 'With the irrational assumption of a core limiting belief clearly identified', watching its ebb and flow in one's mind and then disputing, refuting or questioning it becomes much easier. The process, thereby, removes any mental constrictions for good.

Changing one's paradigms is obviously something that has to be done systematically and frequently, so that the erroneous core beliefs and the underlying, irrational assumptions are permanently eliminated. It calls for changing one's point of view and perspective completely and lastingly. Only then can behaviour that is 'self-limiting' or 'self-sabotaging' be changed.

The process itself is based on questioning the assumptions.

A person has an idea that 'everyone in the audience dislikes me' and is therefore unwilling to speak to them from a lectern.

A way to question this idea is to ask oneself: 'How do you know that everyone dislikes you?' The answer to this question would require further questioning, till one realizes, slowly but surely, that the outside stimuli or situations have nothing much to do with the way one chooses to think and then to behave.

4. 'Practising the process of refuting and dumping' self-limiting beliefs regularly is the final step. The more one does this, the greater are the chances of the irrational beliefs or assumptions being eliminated for good. Then, any event or stimulus is handled in a healthy fashion, and it becomes 'second nature' to respond with full and complete confidence to any kind of event.

We'd like to emphasize that questioning any or all assumptions that we make in the course of our interactions is generally a good thing to do. It helps to keep an open mind that is free from prejudices, which can have a deleterious impact on the way we perceive and engage with the world. It also enables us to be pushed to the limits of our potential, thereby opening the possibilities of living a full and contented life.

Prejudice and Religious Dogma

A person who wishes to experience the taste of sugar does not have to *believe* that sugar has a *particular* taste. The experience of *tasting* will clarify everything, truthfully, the way it is.

The process of searching has to commence with one having an open mind; a mind that is receptive to things *as they are*—not coloured by prior information, borrowed ideas or beliefs that have been handed down. One can choose to be loving and free from preconceived ideas or those that are 'hand-me-downs' from ancient books or even from loved ones who may have inadvertently doled out something to us that has, over time, become a self-limiting belief.

We think that all beliefs—irrespective of their source or the manner in which they have become a part of our thinking patterns—are amenable to the process of evaluation from the perspective of determining whether they are 'helpful' or not. By the term 'helpful' we mean whether they enable the achievement of one's full potential in a way that is free and liberating and which is without any adverse emotional or physical stress or strain to oneself or to others.

Religious beliefs are usually deeply ingrained into the minds of most of us. Such ideas are offered when one is young and impressionable. At that age, one does not rebel against ideas given by others. That has to happen when people start to think critically on their own.

Young boys and girls are often exhorted to believe in, and live their lives, on the basis of certain ideas. Many of these ideas are further fuelled by political, religious or economic considerations; people may be forced to abide by them for fear of ostracism from a community or tribe. Then, the problem of dispensing with flawed beliefs is trickier.

Even when young children grow up and they are fortunate to have acquired the ability to think for themselves and question some of their 'beliefs', there is a deep concern of exclusion from the family or community if the questioning is 'disruptive'. Furthermore, if a person questions a belief, and inquires why something has to be done or not done, then other adherents within a community may resort to manipulating the person by guilt for even demonstrating the temerity of questioning long-held views, beliefs or, what some might label the, 'foundations of our traditions'.

The strong emotions associated with making change or the fear of change and uncertainty makes it even more difficult to 'dispute' or dump religious beliefs and dogma.

Yet to experience the highest truth of life itself, one does not need to 'believe' in anything. Instead, one has to be open and receptive to the process of 'experiencing' life in its entirety on one's own.

Then one is able to live as a 'child of life' upholding all that is life-affirming, wholesome, loving and positive.

Body Language, Authenticity and Effectiveness

In the early 1900s, a German Mathematics teacher and inventor Herr Wilhelm Von Osten owned a horse called Hans. This horse was supposed to have been taught 'math sums' by Von Osten and very quickly acquired the reputation of being able to correctly answer problems of multiplication, division, fractions, subtraction, addition and more. Hans would be asked the question orally or in writing and the horse would always tap the correct answer with one of his front hooves.

Van Osten toured Germany with Clever Hans (der Kluge Hans) and never charged an admission fee for his performances. In 1904, *The New York Times* even wrote an article about this remarkable horse.

What was Hans's secret? When the German Board of Education initiated an investigation, they appointed a 13-person board (aptly called the Hans Commission) to gather evidence. The facts collected were then interpreted by Psychologist Oskar Pfungst.

Pfungst confirmed that Hans would always depend on the questioner's 'body language' to know exactly when to stop tapping his hoof! If the horse could not see the questioner, Hans was unable to perform. The cues from the questioner, though involuntary, were picked up by the alert and intelligent horse!

The beauty about our feelings and emotions is that they show up on our faces and our non-verbal 'body language'. We may try to disguise our feelings (and some people, such as magicians, poker players, actors and charlatans, also succeed in this), but it is not an easy thing to do.

Even when our words attempt to convey something contrary to what we are feeling, our body language gives us away. People and animals (not just Hans) can pick up our non-verbal signals. Besides, people place greater credence on our non-verbal cues rather than on what we may say: So if the two 'tracks' of communication are not congruent, it is your body language that does the 'talking' and you will be viewed suspiciously! But if the congruence is high, then you will be perceived to be authentic, trustworthy and dependable.

People say that leaders that are most loved and respected are the ones who are credible. Their non-verbal and spoken language is completely aligned. The congruence between the spoken word and the corresponding body language is a vital indicator of how 'authentic' one is perceived to be. Authenticity is a sign that you are true to your 'deepest self' and do not allow external situations or conditions to alter what you truly stand for.

(B) Self-esteem and Self-worth

Who am I, Really?

Of the many potent ideas that have a distinct bearing on the quality of the lives we lead, and which determine the nature of our relationships with others, is the way we 'perceive' and 'know' ourselves.

Individuals have asked themselves the question 'Who am I?' for ages. Within this question lies the understanding that we already *exist*, but wish to know our *true nature*: much like little children who have *forgotten* their names and are eager to know their *real* names!

If someone were to ask you the question 'Who are you?', what would you say in response?

The answer to this question would give a fair idea of your 'sense of self' and how you feel about yourself and the many attributes that 'define' you. If our sense of self—our self-image and self-worth—contributes to our being comfortable in our own skin, then it definitely adds to one's well-being and ease. Similarly, an erroneous view of our self, too, would have a strong bearing on how we think and behave.

It would be worthwhile to go through a simple exercise at this stage. Take a pen and a notebook and try and define yourself in words or phrases that do not take recourse to any of the following 'props' to define you: your gender, your family, your neighbourhood, the tribe or caste you are a part of, the town you live in, the schools and colleges you attend or attended or the vocation or job that you are currently involved with.

What you write about yourself is likely to remind you that much like the Sun and the stars, you too are a beautiful, miraculous creation of existence!

What the renowned Philosopher and Jesuit Priest Pierre Teilhard de Chardin (1881–1955) said might help you think about yourself differently:

'We are spiritual beings immersed in a human experience.'

Remembering My True Self

Many years ago a wise woman lived all by herself by the edge of the ocean. She had many wonderful talents and mystical gifts, and people from the nearby villages would come to her to have her heal their sick or to have her bless a new child that had been born. She was loved by one and all and she on her part served everyone with joy and devotion.

After long years, she felt that her body had begun to slow down. She could no longer take care of housework and still attend to the people who would come to visit her. So she decided to get herself a talented attendant who would help her look after the house and give her company.

To get herself help she used her mystical gifts and had the benign ocean provide her with an attendant. The ocean was happy to create a fine, young boy made entirely of salt, sand and water. The boy was the vastness and the magic of the ocean formed into the shape of a young boy.

Though the villagers had no clue where the boy was from, they loved him. They gave him a name. Out of love they would warn him not to go to the ocean, lest he drowns. They got him bright clothes and dressed him up stylishly. Many even started to guess which kingdom he may have come from. Some believed that he was a ship-wrecked sailor who had been washed ashore.

One day, the old woman died. The boy was now older and he felt sad. Between tears he would keep telling the villagers that he had no place to go.

'I am an orphan', he lamented. 'Which village am I from? Who am I?'

The vast ocean heard the lad and laughed at his forgetfulness.

This is a powerful story because it points to our own memory loss when it comes to 'knowing ourselves'. If we are made of the same stuff as the universe, are we not the vastness of the cosmos fashioned into a body? Are we not a unique element of the magic and the mystery that is life itself?

Forgetfulness of our mystical nature begins rather early in our lives. What we think of ourselves is typically based on the acquired 'quality of judgements' and 'emotional evaluations' that are ascribed to us by ourselves and others. What is 'perceived' by us in the course of our interactions with others also plays a part in determining the quality of internalized emotional evaluations.

All such judgements and evaluations—generated by ourselves as well as by those that are proffered by others—are internalized by us from infancy and contribute to the formation of our self-image.

Very often the concept of self is also based on 'props from the past'. These could be labels that others 'attach' to us such as being the grandchild of some notable person or the daughter or spouse of some 'renowned' or 'notorious' individual. This also extends to being associated with a caste, a commune, a tribe or a nation.

What this implies is that the self-image one creates, and the sense of 'worth' that a person feels, is actually a result of what the person is 'told' when the person was a child or what the child inferred from (an obviously child-like interpretation of) its own experiences.

Young children are likely to trust and believe the adults who look after them. So, even when what is told to children is false or only partially right, it is still believed as if it is *entirely* true! Besides, the assumptions and the distinctive experiences of children—mixed with the attendant emotions and feelings that they invariably elicit—also help to frame their unique beliefs, which contribute to their individual self-image and sense of esteem and self-worth.

Getting to one's true self is, therefore, akin to a process of peeling an onion. The layers of judgements and evaluations which have been plastered on us have to be carefully removed, so that we remember our true origins.

I Live as I Perceive Myself

Different families treat their children in very diverse ways. While genetics play a significant role in determining temperament, how children are nurtured and brought-up can be quite impactful.

This diversity—arising from the nurturing environment—creates fertile ground for enormous variations in the manner in which children, with otherwise similar gifts, perceive themselves. This is over and above the ways children feel about their own bodies, their minds, their tendencies to relate with others and so on. There are also countless emotions that are spontaneously generated within a growing child's mind and that colour the child's perceptions. Comparisons with others, too, generate their own emotions.

The perceptions we create and hold about ourselves are elements of our self-image. Our self-image has the potential to affect our behaviour throughout our lives, even as adults.

Since the sum total of all our thoughts and experiences together determine the choices we make and how we behave, the trajectory of our lives is clearly an outcome of our self-image.

If children have been provided emotional evaluations about themselves by their elders—especially those elders who were important to them and whom they *viewed* as being significant and trustworthy—then they are likely to treat the bulk of such ideas about themselves as being true. Such inputs would become a part of their self-perceptions, thereby colouring their beliefs.

These beliefs could focus on values the person stands for, what they think they are good at and what they are not so accomplished at. These varied inputs—if not disputed and questioned or changed in time—tend to get 'ossified' and hardened into firmly held beliefs about oneself. These beliefs would also give rise to emotions that become a part of the personality traits of the children and remain 'embedded'—like hardened blobs of resin—in their psyche, right into adulthood.

One might wonder: Why would parents or loving elders wilfully ever tell their child things that can 'scar' the child's sense of self-worth?

This is not an easy question to answer. For one, human interactions are complex and myriad other factors aggravate or accentuate certain traits in adults, which bear on the family environment. This in turn creates an ambience—sometimes wholesome, often dysfunctional, and with all kinds of possible nuanced variations in between—within which young children learn to function and cope. Second, irrespective of what the parents or the child's elders might do or say in the course of a child's growing years, the child too comes with its own judgement. Therefore, the child—not unlike adults—might 'interpret' a set of perfectly normal, and natural 'parental behaviours' as being directed *against* its interests. This can lead to further patterns being formed in the child's mind. If left undisputed or if not jettisoned from the mind altogether, such ideas can create behaviour that can come in the way of being able to relate effectively with others.

So, apart from judgements made by elders, emotional evaluations are also abundantly offered by one's own tendencies. The 'emotional evaluations' and the 'self-talk' that these yield are a major contributor to one's sense of self.

Self-talk and Self-perception

Self-talk occurs when we think and articulate our ideas for ourselves. Nobody can hear our self-talk because it is in our heads.

The following 'thoughts' are examples of self-talk:

'I'm very beautiful.'
'My pimples make me ugly.'
'I am the great granddaughter of the Queen of Vilnius.'
'I have the biggest house on this street.'
'My car is a $500,000 Ferrari. Is yours even close?'
'I'm a saint compared to my dipsomaniac friends.'
'People just love my sense of dress and fashion.'
'I have the smarts to do well in any job.'
'I just can't cook (or ride a bike, sing, dance, do Sudoku, crosswords…) and I hate myself!'
'She's smarter than me and has a more caring boy-friend than mine.'
'I'm the only one in my class who hasn't yet made love to a boy/girl. I'm a loser!'
'Everyone is so happy in their marriage! Look at me, I've got such a bad deal!'

All these statements are ideas that people hold about themselves. Many of these statements might be completely false, but the thinkers *believe* in them! The thoughts emanate from the beliefs that persons have about themselves.

The bitter truth is that without exercising the power of the discriminating intellect, the human mind has the quality of internalizing and clinging to everything that the mind throws up. Without the application of our intellect, our minds do not know how to differentiate between what is true and what is not! So anything that emerges as a thought and then is stated as self-talk—anything really, which may either be a pure fact or pure fiction or bits of fact and fiction mixed together—is internalized and accepted as a fact.

When irrational or limiting thoughts (and corresponding self-talk) first lodge in our minds, they can either be disputed or reinforced, with self-talk emanating from the intellect. For instance, if a young woman catches herself thinking 'I'm a loser!', she can *reflect* on this thought and dispute it by questioning herself, using the appropriate self-talk:

'Why do I say I'm a loser?' (Rational Questioning, RQ)
'It's Friday and I'm sitting at home watching a sitcom, when all my friends are out having fun with their friends.' (Response to the question above)
'Are you sure *all* your friends are out? Besides, if you've chosen to be home on Friday, why does that make you a loser?' (More RQ)
'Well, maybe not all my friends..., but look why am I not out having fun?'
'Yes, why are you not out with your friends? Why did you decline the invitation that you got from your colleagues to join them at the bowling alley?' (RQ)
'Well, umm....'

After the above dialogue—with the rational questioning taken to its logical end—chances are the young woman will no longer use the phrase 'I'm a loser!' as part of her self-talk again! The erroneous, irrational thought pattern would have been dumped with the help of the rational questioning. However, if the process remains incomplete and the woman still thinks that she is a loser just because she is at home on a Friday night, then this flawed idea would be stored in her mind and could become a part of how she perceives herself.

All ideas and thoughts contribute to the creation—within every person's mind—of the *ego*. The ego is a *false identity* of *ourselves* that we are responsible for creating, based on all the stuff that we receive and internalize from the time we are about two years of age.

It is worth noting that the ego gets created well after a child's birth. It is not something that we are born with.

Eat, My Long, Beautiful Sleeves, Eat!

We call the ego a 'false identity', because it does not define you truly.

In the fourteenth century, there lived a wise and revered mystic in Kashmir, who was called Nunde-Rishi. One day, a rich merchant implored Nunde-Rishi to visit his house for dinner to celebrate the success of one of his ventures. At first Nunde-Rishi declined, but when the merchant started wailing and crying and threatening that he would kill himself on the spot if the holy man refused to visit his home and be his chief guest, the compassionate mystic agreed to attend the dinner.

On the appointed day, the merchant's house was all agog in anticipation of the party that evening. From the crack of dawn, a dozen cooks and their assistants got busy preparing the choicest delicacies for the elaborate and sumptuous menu that had been planned.

By sundown, the guests started to arrive. Governors of neighbouring lands, judges and commanders of the realm, wealthy merchants with their wives and children and the most accomplished dancers and courtesans, all came in their finery. All were ushered into the big hall that had been especially lit with torches of burning and fragrant pinewood resin. The guards at the door made sure that all the dignitaries were welcomed within, while the urchins, the common folk and the beggars were warded off with angry words, curses and the thwack of their batons.

When Nunde-Rishi arrived at the merchant's home, he was dressed in a plain *pheran* (a long, traditional woollen gown worn in Kashmir) that slung over his simple, drab clothes. The host, not recognizing him, sent him away threatening to send his guards to clobber him hard if he kept insisting that he was meant to be at the dinner.

It was now time to serve dinner. Nunde-Rishi was not to be seen anywhere in the hall. The merchant was getting agitated. He wanted the mystic to bless the meal before the guests could eat.

It was then that someone discovered the grave mistake. Nunde-Rishi had wrongly been sent away! The poor merchant almost died of fear and contrition, but upon being encouraged he ran out to locate Nunde-Rishi and found him wandering peacefully in the woods nearby.

The merchant begged for forgiveness and entreated the amused Nunde-Rishi to join the feast. Nunde-Rishi agreed.

But before setting out, the mystic did something dramatic. He discarded his pheran and wore an exquisite gold embroidered, long-sleeved habiliment that he pulled out of a small bag. Then he combed his hair, adorned himself with the most fragrant perfume and then set out with the merchant.

When Nunde-Rishi, the chief guest at the feast, finally sat down with the guests to enjoy the lavish dinner, he placed his long sleeves on the food in front of him and said:

'Eat, my long, beautiful sleeves, eat!'

Nunde-Rishi was making a very simple yet profound point that we still have difficulty understanding; namely, all that our ego identifies with (in this story, the trappings of wealth, power, prestige and obviously fine clothes) is *unreal*.

The *unreal* ego is acquired through a person's interactions with the world. As time goes by, one erroneously starts to believe that the ego is the 'real self'. In fact, a question that enlightened sages have always used to prompt clearer thinking in this area is whether we can 'describe who we are without taking recourse to our past, our assets, our relationships, our likely future or to our current profession'.

The exercise that you were introduced to at the start of this section was based on this very powerful idea.

What such an exercise helps us to do is to come nearer and nearer to the truth that defines us in our purest, most pristine forms—devoid of labels from the past or from identities that stem from being a part of a commune, a faith, a profession or a nation. Even one's profession cannot be a prop or a hook by which to define one's true self.

There is a 'true self' beyond the ego, and that is what one has to recognize to have genuine self-worth. In fact, that self which mystics and enlightened seers have often simply hinted towards by using the term 'I am' to define it, is all that we have when we manifest in the realm of our planet.

Think of this 'I am'—the consciousness of your being alive—as the 'real part of you'. Something akin to a 'spirit field': within your bodies and surrounding it. That which was born with your arrival on Earth and which is the pure and unblemished mirror-like *consciousness* that reflects everything that is perceived. The 'dust' of interactions sometimes hides the self and we forget who we really are.

Our Egos Colour Reality

In the early twentieth century, Emperor Puyito of China was determined to stop the demeaning practice that Han men were subjected to by earlier Qing dynasty conquerors. To enable all enslaved Han men to be easily pulled into subjugation, the conquerors had made it mandatory for them all to wear their hair long, with a braided pony tail dangling from their heads. This *queue*, as it was called, was therefore a sign of slavery.

Yet, since the practice had been on for so long, when Emperor Puyito asked his people to get rid of something that smacked of servility, they refused to do so, reacting violently to the emperor's suggestion!

An erroneous sense of self can definitely be limiting to one's well-being. If one's world view gets distorted due to an erroneous 'self-image' that one carries within oneself, it can cause undue stress, poor relationships and a range of negative emotions from even ordinary interactions.

There is, therefore, great merit in dumping the false sense of identity (one's ego) that can come in the way of living a life of peace, well-being and contentment. In that sense, the false identity is also akin to an erroneous set of programmes being carried in one's mind, which needs to be treated the way we would treat beliefs that are self-limiting; that is, by eliminating them: lock, stock and barrel.

Considerable stress and discomfort are experienced by people who erroneously have identified with limiting notions about themselves. Such people may also demonstrate an inability to set high goals and then work towards achieving them, because the underlying beliefs will serve as a powerful limiting factor to anything that they might wish to do in the pursuit of those goals.

Therefore, changing one's erroneous ideas about oneself is absolutely essential. In an earlier section, we also spoke about disputing such beliefs. That process is equally applicable to beliefs or ideas about oneself and one's identity and self-esteem.

Many people go through their lives making no effort to change those limiting conditions or beliefs that they carry within their minds all the time. More than any factor outside, the 'inner dimension'—our interiority—plays a pivotal role in the sense of fulfilment that we experience in life.

The ego is one of the most powerful deceptions that our minds conjure. We identify with the ego from fairly early in our lives, and invest in strengthening it and making its envelope-like hold on the underlying 'I am' even stronger than before.

Why It Is So Difficult to Dislodge the Ego

Any kind of transformation is not easy. This is especially true of our egos. Reducing its authority over us is tough. Yet, it needs to be done for our own well-being and joy.

A part of the problem is that we associate so intensely with the dust and the grime of conditioning on the pure mirror of our interiority that we begin to *invest* more and more of our emotional energy into all that, which reinforces the false image that we have of ourselves. We actually begin to *believe* that we are the way the conditioning suggests we are!

Any attempt by anyone outside of us to change any part of this false identity is bound to be resisted and can result in violent reactions as well. If a part of our own selves wishes to change something, we are quite likely to delude ourselves by saying such things as: 'I'm fine the way I am' or 'The problem I'm facing has to do with A, who is tormenting me! I don't need to change.'

Much of the misery and the troubles one gets to experience in this world stem from an intense identification with one's ego and the emotional troubles that arise when one identifies with something that is intrinsically false, coloured (based on biases or judgemental evaluations) or impermanent.

Take for instance the concept of one's religious faith. For most of us, just being born in a certain family or community determines the faith that we 'grow up with'. This constitutes a thick layer of conditioning. All the rituals and the dos and don'ts that are associated with the world's many faiths, which are 'imposed' on us as children, provide a solid covering on our true selves.

We gradually contribute to this layer even more by adding to it more sheaths made up of our own ideas and constructs. We 'invest in strengthening' the layers, because we actually come to believe that our sense of self is inseparable from that thick layer of conditioning. The same applies to many of our faith-based beliefs as well. We may be atheists, but even that is a 'decal' stuck onto our selves. We go to great lengths to strengthen the hold of many such labels of conditioning onto ourselves.

We then identify with the ego that is created and supported by the same 'decals' of conditioning. We associate too much of ourselves with the ego, and any attempt to dislodge or change the tags creates fear, trepidation and anger, because of the concern that we would lose our identity if that were to happen.

The anger generated by a suggestion to change can be so intense that it can lead to violence, riots and even wars. Worse still, there can be prolonged hatred of communities or nations for one another.

Living one's life on the basis of the grime, the dust and the proffered stickers on our minds—that obscures a view of our true self—can only cause misunderstandings, conflict and absence of peaceful interactions. If you explore the conditionings deeper, you would find that many of the ideas that cover our true selves are false. Events from the lives of individuals and of nations around the world bear testimony to this: People operating from their egos, their false identities, are unable to see things without the tints and distortions of their own decals, thereby causing conflict, agitation and pain.

When we understand that one's 'inner world' needs to be cleansed of extraneous conditioning to expose our true selves, then we are on the path to reach our full potential. The process of *understanding* that all of us 'are not' necessarily all that others have repeatedly told us needs patience, perseverance and practice to internalize. This process of *reflection* and *meditation* by the 'watcher' in you alone helps remove the false ego forever.

In that sense, this process is not so much about changing of one's personality to develop a 'new self' as much as a process of *revealing* one's *true* personality.

When we experience our true self, we know.

Making Change That Is Not Superficial

An ancient Indian tale from the *Panchatantra* tells us about a wild donkey that felt clumsy and stupid in the presence of his other friends, who would always scare the poor beast away and prevent it from grazing.

Despondent, dejected and hungry, the donkey undertook a journey to get away from his friends, so that he could graze in peace, and not experience feelings of hurt and anger. He walked for many a day till he came to the edge of the forest.

While he was resting under a tree, he noticed a number of vultures feeding on something a short distance away. Curious, the donkey ambled to the spot and discovered that the carrion birds had been feeding on the carcass of a lion. The skin of the king of the jungle was still intact. The donkey then hit upon an idea. He would wear the lion's skin and that would scare away all the other beasts—including his friends—and he could then graze to his heart's delight.

So that's what the donkey did. He returned to his part of the forest wearing the skin of the lion and frightened all the foolish animals that he encountered. His friends bolted away the moment they saw what looked like a lion coming towards them, and thereafter, the donkey enjoyed grazing in the green meadows without anyone disturbing him.

One day, the donkey was so elated with his new-found state of contentment that he spontaneously started to bray. At that moment, the beasts understood that he was a donkey wearing a lion's skin and quickly forced him out of the forest.

Making meaningful and lasting change is more than just donning a different skin. The donkey was motivated to make some change because he was unable to graze and would have starved if it couldn't.

For most of us, unless there are overwhelming reasons to change, we seldom do. Yet making improvements is essential to be able to reach one's full potential and leading a life that is productive and joyful.

We think there are four main reasons for most of us not committing to lasting change.

The first is that it is so *much easier* for people to depend on what others tell them, rather than to take responsibility for their own lives. It is far more comfortable to listen to a teacher and go on with one's life, rather than working on oneself, identifying the dust and patches, scraping them off and embarking on the arduous process of ultimately ripping off any conditioning that might be limiting our lives by covering our true selves.

The second reason is that we 'delude ourselves' into believing that any and all the 'problems' that make our lives tough or unpleasant are 'out there', on the outside, and beyond our control. The descriptions that we have stuck onto *our* minds colour our world view and determine the way we interact with the outside. These conditionings prevent an unsullied interpretation of our reality, making it easy for us to blame the outside for our troubles.

The third reason is that 'much emotional energy has been invested' in the false reality, as well as in the conditions and outcomes of holding on to that view. Any departure from that seems like an unproductive U-turn from all that we may have done throughout our lives!

Changing anything about ourselves can be painful. Hence, it cannot happen without unwavering commitment, patience and diligence. Which is why having a supportive and encouraging group of people to assist us in the process of change is desirable and beneficial.

The fourth and final reason why it is difficult to make lasting change is the fact that 'it entails taking a risk'. Changing something that we are comfortable with involves pushing the boundaries of our comfort zones. It also necessitates operating in a region of unfamiliar interactions and trying out new ways of engaging with the wider world. This could be scary for many of us.

The worry of being ostracized by one's near and dear friends and family members, when one changes, is also a dampener that stymies people from taking a corrective plunge. In that sense, the possibility of being ridiculed is also a potential risky outcome of change and one has to fortify oneself for such things. It is quite normal for loved ones to react—often negatively—to any changes one might notice in the behaviour of someone who has been known for a long time; or if such a person is someone whose behaviour is now no longer predictable. Such a response from close friends and family is quite normal!

Friends and family are also very likely to question a person's decision to change; even if it means that the person who has changed is happier and is feeling less burdened and more fulfilled.

This is a tipping point. If a person gets to this stage, it is a good indication that the transformational journey might indeed continue.

(C) Being Present and Mindful

Life Unfurls in the Now!

All 'life' unfurls in the 'present moment' alone! Life's many beautiful miracles manifest only in the 'now'; if we are not mindful of the present moment and are not fully present in the 'now' and 'here', we will be disconnected from life itself! We will be 'nowhere'!

Think about this. We can only live and be alive now! Whatever we may have experienced until now remains with us merely in the form of memories. Memories are just traces in our minds.

The future, if we think about it, is not the future. It is just a *thought* about what might happen at some future 'now' moment! The future can only happen when it becomes a 'now'.

That is why 'now' is equated with both 'life' and 'eternity'. The notions of the 'past' and the 'future' are ideas created in our own minds, which links events together to give the semblance of 'moving time'.

Our mind has the ability to remember events from a previous 'now', which it juxtaposes in the context of another event happening in another 'now'. This creates the illusion of a stream of events. We call this an illusion, because it is precisely that. It is our minds that attach the different scenes—stored in our intricate memories—into one, seamless continuum and make it seem to us that there is a linear progression of time. In effect, our past memories and their retrieval by our minds, and their projection into the future, create the notion of time! If the mind forgets the past (as some patients of dementia experience), their understanding is always of their current perceptions.

This idea can be unsettling, but we would like that you let the logic of what is being stated lead you to your own understanding of this important concept.

This does not mean that the earth does not rotate on its axis or that the sun does not rise or set. But even the notion of an Earth day, one that we call 'today', being different from a day that we have termed 'yesterday' comes from the remarkable qualities of our own minds.

We can go a step further. The light emanating from a distant star within the galactic core of the Milky Way galaxy reaches our eyes 'now'. So in our perception the event is happening now: because our senses and our minds—working together—create this (erroneous and false) impression of reality.

In actuality, the starlight may have left the distant star 35,000 Earth-years ago (the galactic core of our galaxy is about 35,000 light years away from our Sun) and it has only reached us now! So we believe that an event is occurring now, when in reality it has occurred a long, long time ago. Our senses and our minds together, therefore, do distort the truth and make us believe things that might be false.

The Tricks Our Minds Play

We all see things as our minds wish us to see them.

This is why a wise lady once observed that the world is not full of 'things', but 'thinks'!

Because of the remarkable qualities of the human mind and our amazing sense organs, we are perpetually interpreting our life experiences on the basis of what is perceived by our imperfect senses and then stored in our minds. We do not, as a rule, gather all our experiences directly in the present moment. Besides, we cannot always be sure that our experience has been sans any distortions due to imperfect sensory inputs, mindless distractions, past conditionings, erroneous perceptions or stored biases. The lens of our flawed perceptions and strong conditionings together distort our world view, and we actually come to 'believe' and operate from the 'disfigured reality'.

Pablo Picasso, the famous and influential Spanish artist, was once travelling in a train when a well-known and successful Spanish businessman struck a conversation with him.

The businessman introduced himself and then told Picasso that while he appreciated his success, his paintings needed improvement!

So, beauty is indeed in the eye of the beholder!

Our senses are known to deceive us, because our sense organs (along with the master controller, the brain) have evolved with the primary endeavour of ensuring our survival. The sense organs are effective when they are used to register only significant, comparative differences in the range within which they are effective. Therefore, using our eyes, we might notice differences in colour or brightness. But we cannot distinguish very well between minor differences of the same colour or differing levels of brightness. Similarly, we might feel something mildly warm with very cold hands, and think that it is hot. Using our hands we would also be unable to ascribe a precise temperature to tepid water, because our senses in tandem with our brains work on comparisons not absolutes.

Furthermore, our sense organs need our minds to be fully alert and working to be able to help us make meaning of our experiences. If a person is asleep, for instance, and someone forcibly opens the sleeper's eyelids and places a beautiful red rose before the opened eyes, the sleeper is unlikely to remember seeing a rose at all! The eyes would have functioned without a flaw, but the effect is as if the eyes 'saw' nothing at all! No wonder bystanders who have witnessed a crime scene are unable to precisely share what they saw or heard, because the mind was too perturbed to enable the senses to register the 'reality' of the event.

This interesting phenomenon demonstrates that even as our sense organs are affected by external stimuli, they do not register the meaning or the import of the stimulus unless the mind is *alert* and *fully receptive* to the sense inputs in the 'now'.

Stored memories and the emotions associated with them also deceive us by creating a number of filters or lenses. These filters selectively strain out or alter valuable information and make our present experiences less enriching, or grotesquely unreal. Worse still, just the memory of painful or fearful events, which may have occurred at some previous moment, can badly affect our well-being in the present. This is not just debilitating but can adversely affect our abilities in the present and hamper our work and leisure activities.

Ideas, the traces of past events in our minds or the memories of painful or intense emotions, therefore, create blocks which colour or even alter our perceptions. This makes us less receptive to diverse ideas, opinions or perspectives that differ from our own mental models, representational systems (rep-systems) or presumed 'world view'. We might also create patterns or imagine sinister plots or conspiracies being played out, even though these may just be projections of our own minds, with no connection or bearing with the stimuli received in the present moment.

It is said that what we focus on in our minds, grows. Therefore, if we focus on only the negative and hateful news that we receive, we might not see the good or the love that exists in our world as well.

Having our minds completely and fully present—here and now—and totally free from mind filters are essential for a complete and unsullied experience.

Which Wolf Are You Feeding?

This is a lovely Cherokee story.

An old chief was teaching his grandson about life.

'A fight is going on inside me,' he told the young boy, 'a fight between two wolves.'

The young lad was listening attentively.

'One wolf is full of anger, sorrow, regret, greed, self-pity and false pride.

The other is focused in the now, full of joy, peace, love, humility, kindness and faith.'

'This same fight is going on inside of you, grandson…and inside of every other person on the face of this earth.'

The grandson dwelt on this for a moment and then asked, 'Grandfather, which wolf will win?'

The old man smiled and said, 'The one that you feed.'

'Feeding the wolf' is a metaphor for allowing ourselves to direct our minds to a chosen state that could either be a state of peace, hope and well-being, or the opposite. It matters in life what we focus our minds on and the wolf we wish to feed.

If we let any of our anxieties that afflict our minds to dominate our thinking, then we are feeding the wrong wolf. This has another consequence: Remembering hurtful past events, or worrying about future outcomes, prevents us from experiencing life wholesomely in the present. In the 'now and here', we experience things as they are in their truest forms. Our imperfect senses are still at play, but with a mind that is feeding neither wolf, there is quiescence. We are alert, mindful and receptive to all that is happening in the present.

Being aware, or mindful, is another way of saying that one is totally *present*. In such a state, you recognize, remember and then experience that you are an integral part of the mysteries and the miracles that are life!

Yes, the many miracles of life are all around you! Your own body is a miracle. Your breathing, the constant pumping of your heart, the circulation of your bloodstream, the way your body fights pathogens all the time! These things happen without any conscious help from you. For example, a tiny seed sprouting from the earth to form a seedling and then growing further to become a resplendent flowering plant or a source of nutritious food. If these are not miracles, then what is?

Being present and mindful—as a healthy habit—can bring great joy and peace of mind because all the stress we carry is usually a result of us regretting our *past* or worrying about our *future*. The present can never induce stress because you can be and act only in the present! The mind is not juggling thoughts and faux actions related to the past or the future.

Another benefit of being mindful is that it makes us a steadfast *witness* of all that is happening within and without us. This ability to become a *watcher* of all that we are doing, as we engage with our external environment, gives us a chance to gauge how we think.

Once we observe ourselves, as well as the stimuli that direct our thoughts in certain ways, it opens up a window of possibilities for us to *choose* how we think. Over time, as our practice of *mindfulness* becomes 'full-bodied', we can also observe if there are any beliefs that are automatically causing us to feel a certain way when triggered by stimuli. Being mindful is a beautiful way of preventing us from falling prey to an 'amygdala hijack' and of feeding the wrong wolf!

Getting Off the Horse

There is a beautiful Zen story that we both like.

One day, a man on a galloping horse thundered past a group of people in the town square. It was evident that the rider was eager to reach someplace, possibly before a critical deadline.

'Where are you going, friend?' a curious onlooker shouted at the rider.

'I don't know!' said the man in a hurry, 'Ask the horse!'

The horse in this elegantly simple story represents the habitual working of the mind. Like a horse that is wayward, our minds too wander. Our habitual train of thoughts is truly akin to a group of horses pulling our minds—and our attention—away from the present.

If you are listening to someone, and the person speaks of something that you are familiar with, chances are that even as the person is talking, your mind and attention would have 'flitted away' to the zone where you are reliving some experience—the memories of which were triggered by the speaker!

Anything that the speaker would have said while your mind was wandering may have been heard by your ears, but it would not have registered much of it at all! Not being mindful of this fact and not practising being 'now and here' makes us 'mindless', distracted and inattentive. This, in turn, makes us prone to committing errors of various kinds, including serious errors of judgement.

The surest way to be *present* and in the 'now' at all times is to be conscious of the twin phenomena of 'mind wandering' and 'thought hijacking'. Whenever the mind wanders, one has to gently, and with awareness, bring the mind back to the present. In that state, one also has to cultivate awareness of one's self—one's body, the feelings that arise from time to time and one's surroundings. This will heighten the receptivity of the senses and ensure that by being fully in the present, we grasp whatever is happening comprehensively and with complete attention.

Thought hijacking occurs when a thought that surfaces in our minds takes us on a creative spin in a totally different direction, where we move absent-mindedly into a different realm, far away from the present. Being mindful of this can take us from mind wandering to the eternal 'now'.

It also helps to focus on one's breathing and 'watching' one's breath as it flows into one's nostrils during inhalation and out again. This approach has a very calming effect on one's mind too, because in the 'here and now' the mind cannot dredge painful thoughts out of the past or invite scary, imagined concerns of the future. It is this habit of flitting back and forth, with the horse of our minds leading us, which ordinarily stresses our minds and gives rise to many psychosomatic ailments and considerable emotional and physical *dis-ease*.

Having a calm mind is a prerequisite for being *present*. If the mind is agitated and in distress, it is obviously enslaved by the emotions and the thoughts that are bubbling up and causing the distress. Learning to operate with a calm mind at all times is therefore essential. The beauty is by being in the present; the stillness of the mind is further 'fortified', reinforcing greater ease and comfort.

Being fully *present*, and totally in the now, is also the essence of being *meditative*, and mindful. An ensuing calm mind unleashes capabilities in the 'now'. This also ensures heightened personal effectiveness, because as you know, all human achievements occur in the 'now'!

Mindfulness Meditative Practices

Being mindful means being present in a situation fully. It also means being a *witness* to one's own self, one's own thinking processes, speech and behaviour.

It is possible to be mindful, or *consciously aware*, of our own thinking. Yes, it is you who is thinking, but a part of you can, nonetheless, dispassionately look at the way your thinking patterns result in emotions, feelings and reactions to external stimuli.

Being mindful is also a potent way to be present and not anywhere else because of our thinking. In the present, we can also distinguish between inputs that we receive in the present moment—from external stimuli generated 'now'—and the evaluations and judgemental interpretations that are inadvertently imposed on these events by our mind. This ability to watch and then distinguish between a 'neutral' occurrence (such as a cat stealthily catching a bird and then feeding upon it) and your awareness of the feelings it generates in you is a powerful way to *choose* your responses to all kinds of diverse situations.

One can actually discern that while the act of the cat eating the bird is a natural thing in the animal world, your reaction and the feelings that observing the event might generate in you are due only to your own ideas and judgements being imposed on the event. As has been explained earlier in this chapter, a 'belief' is a representation, a pattern in a person's mind about certain ideas, that the person considers true. Somewhat like an *ersatz* reality or an image of what that person considers real.

Some of the mindfulness meditative practices that are now followed around the world are aimed at helping people to learn how to be present and completely in the 'now'; that is, in the present moment. With practice, this enables us to understand that our responses to stimuli are completely due to the thinking patterns and beliefs that reside in our own minds.

Simple Techniques to Cultivate Mindfulness

There are many effective, meditative techniques that have been tried out for thousands of years in India. Some scholars claim that there are at least 108 documented methods of meditation, and of making the mind still, so as to be wholly present at all times.

One of these powerful techniques—popularised by Siddhartha Gautama, the Buddha—was propounded by him as a part of his own personal experience of the truth nearly 2,500 years ago. The technique is known as *vipassana* which literally means 'seeing things as they are, with clear insight'. This technique is taught by a number of spiritual masters around the globe to this day.

Broadly, the technique consists of first helping one to calm one's mind through a process known as *samatha*. Samatha is the Pali term for the Sanskrit word *Sammādhi* that is a process of establishing a state of concentration and focusing the mind to remain still and unwavering. In Buddhist literature, it is mentioned that samatha enables the mind to become tranquil.

When samatha ensures that the mind is calm and relaxed, the second stage involves witnessing or vipassana. Regular practice with the twin processes helps one to learn to be 'calm and watchful' at all times. One begins to be a watcher, a witness, who *non-judgementally* experiences everything that occurs in the present moment with full awareness. The witnessing even extends to whatever might be happening *within* a person's body–mind and not just to events outside of one's body.

To begin the practice of vipassana, it helps to watch one's breath emanating from the nose and being fully conscious and mindful of the manner in which the air moves in and out of one's nostrils. This focused attention has to be practised daily, and for longer and longer durations, so that irrespective of what one might be doing one can be mindful and present.

With the passage of time, one can also practise 'mindful eating', 'mindful walking' and so on. In fact, ultimately, everything should be done mindfully, so that we are ever present and in the here and now. Eating food, listening to another person in a one-to-one conversation or just walking in a garden alone are ideal activities to start with, so that over time you can bring more and more of your waking life into the ambit of mindfulness.

Being meditative and mindful actually means being fully present in the magical unfurling of life.

Four Steps to Mindfulness

To respond to situations of all kinds in a more mindful way, the following four steps have been known to help:

Step 1. Breathing rhythmically—Maintaining evenly paced breathing is essential, with an in and out rhythm that is comfortable. By focusing on our breathing, we bring our thinking under control. We may eliminate thoughts that roil us up, releasing them with each breath. By focusing on our breathing, we regain our attention and concentration.

Step 2. Being aware of our body—With each breath, we become more aware of our body. We bring our responses of the moment under control. We direct our attention towards our face getting flushed, our palms getting sweaty, our skin getting goosebumps or our ire being raised. With focus on our breathing, we also bring our body into a steady state, calming our systems down.

Step 3. Releasing tension—With each breath and a raised level of awareness, we bring ourselves into control and release pent-up tensions. We let go and become more centred in who we really are. Releasing tension returns us to our principles and calmer ways of interacting.

Step 4. Raising attentiveness—As we maintain our inner calmness and strength, we listen to what is being said more intently and we watch the way in which it is being said. We become more aware as we empathise with the other. Our raised attentiveness enables us to respond more thoughtfully and, if needed, begin to direct the exchange in a direction of collaboration or other productive areas of discussion.

Awareness, Acceptance and Gratitude

Awareness, as we have shared with you, requires bringing one's mind gently back each time it wanders, and then, training it to be tranquil and in the 'here and now'—the present—at all times. That's one part.

The other part is not to impose any of one's preferences, likes or dislikes upon the reality that is being experienced. This is the meaning of demonstrating non-judgemental understanding or *acceptance* of whatever is being experienced.

An occurrence, or an event that you may be witnessing, can elicit feelings and thoughts based on your own, prior evaluations of similar situations. Not being judgemental is not always easy, because one's prejudices, preferences, likes and dislikes are deeply embedded in our minds and act swiftly on anything that we notice or observe. Besides, when we see or experience an event, we label it in a way that enables us to deal with it automatically (remember, our brain is designed by the forces of evolution to ensure our survival). So when our senses give us a signal, there is this immediate desire to label it and associate an evaluative opinion with it.

If our conditioned beliefs or preferences are allowed to impinge on the stimuli, then within nanoseconds one can generate a completely imagined representation of the experienced reality. This, in turn, can create considerable negativity or stress (or both) in the perceiver of the experience. In fact, much of the stress created in our lives is on account of the 'automatic' reactions to stimuli (see the Section on 'Thinking, Feeling and Behaving' for details) generated when our erroneous beliefs work on inputs collated by our senses. Belief-based triggers are known as 'automatic thoughts' because they kick in almost instantaneously after a stimulus is received!

Being judgemental, therefore, means to be a slave to these automatic thoughts. Vipassana requires that the subject (you) witnesses the objective reality with absolutely no distortions imposed by the mind. If anything, feelings of gratitude and love can reside in our hearts, as these heighten awareness and bring about a transformation in any negative beliefs that might be embedded in our minds.

It has been said that 'love is the total and complete acceptance of what is'. Therefore, when we sensitize our senses and our minds to being loving and grateful, we are very likely to stop judging. The process of practising non-judging becomes easier with all the benefits accruing to us as we spend more and more time doing it. Finally, here is a prayer of gratitude, by an unknown author, which we find uplifting.

Be thankful that you don't already have everything you desire...if you did, what would there be to look forward to?

Be thankful when you don't know something...for it gives you the opportunity to learn.

Be thankful for the difficult times...during those times you grow.

Be thankful for your limitations…they give you opportunities for improvement.

Be thankful for each new challenge…which will build your strength and character.

Be thankful for your mistakes…they will teach you valuable lessons.

Be thankful when you're tired and weary…because it means you've given your all.

It's easy to be thankful for the 'good' things…yet, a life of rich fulfilment comes to those who are thankful for the setbacks.

Gratitude can turn a negative into a positive. Find a way to be thankful for your troubles and they can become your blessings.

(D) Choice and Accountability

Making Choices, Shaping Destiny

Life is a mysterious, yet beautiful gift. How we live it is a *choice* each one of us makes. How today will turn out is up to me. This is because we have the gift of free will.

There is an element of chance in what life might proffer in the form of 'life's circumstances'. But beyond that, on a daily basis, each one of us can exercise choices to enable us to navigate through life's unknown journey in a way that is joyful, rewarding and fulfilling.

We do have the power to exercise choices in the present, the 'now'. Nobody is a puppet at the end of a chain being controlled by a supernatural force. Luck, providence and destiny might play a role in one's life, but we need to appreciate that one's volition plays a significant part as well.

Disregarding the power of choices that we may exercise robs us of the myriad opportunities for growth. It also prevents us from reaching our potential. Besides, opportunities for growth often come disguised in one's life as 'problems' or 'decision points', which force us to make choices.

Guidance on what the right choices might be in a given situation is discernible from the way we *feel* at the time we make a decision. Our inner world or our *interiority*—which is the invisible space that forms the most important part of our personalities—is the place where we alone experience our deepest feelings. This space is also a powerful source of guidance for each of us. The lighter and more joyful we feel within ourselves when we do something is an indication that the action is aligned with Life. If something unsettles or stresses you, chances are that it is not right for you at that moment.

However, in a world full of noise and excessive sensory stimulation, this inner space and the intelligent voice of wisdom and guidance that emanates from it is often drowned out. We need to learn to consciously practise being quiet, still and silent, if this source of infallible insight is to be tapped.

The Twins—Choice and Accountability

Accountability refers to the internal, cognitive processes by which an individual makes a *personal choice* to take *ownership* of some, or all aspects of a task or situation, to achieve a set of intended results.

By choosing a certain outcome, an individual commits internal resources to reach the goal. Thereafter, managing diverse aspects of the situation and relationships with others appropriately, one would ensure a high probability of reaching the desired outcome.

Accountability differentiates the whiners from the problem-solvers.

Even if, for some reason, the results achieved are not as expected, the individual would neither lapse into a state of feeling like a victim of circumstances, nor start *blaming* all and sundry for the debacle. Instead, accountable persons would emphatically state that the 'buck stopped at their desks' and would proceed to determine the reasons for the lapse. They would also ensure that the learning from such a review would be applied to prevent a recurrence of possible failures in future. As we mentioned earlier, no whining!

Accountability is a critical aspect of individual and collective well-being, because it places the 'locus of control' for one's thoughts, emotions and actions squarely on oneself. This orientation helps a person stay 'in control' and remain in a state of creative problem-solving even as life's myriad situations unfurl. By focusing on 'what one can do', rather than moping about one's circumstances, one feels energized and effective.

Besides, when teams are involved in getting a task done, if all people work with accountability, the team quickly self-regulates, placing emphasis on the desired group norms, and the performance standards. The team's collective outcome remains in focus and the likelihood of success at the task is greatly enhanced thereby.

Accountability exercised as a personal choice by all team members helps to forge cohesive teamwork, eliminates blaming, enables peak performance and helps the group to cohesively make continuous improvements in the process for even better results in the next round.

The I and They Factors

One's temperament and attitude towards life make a huge difference to the manner in which one lives. Research from around the world shows that happiness and a sense of achievement have a lot to do with a person's own attitude. In fact, it is commonly said about success in careers that 'attitude gives altitude'. Abraham Lincoln is believed to have said: 'We can complain because rose bushes have thorns, or rejoice because thorn bushes have roses.'

The orientations that we have towards life's circumstances, objects, people or situations, as well as the choices we make in life, are a key determinant of attitude. If we *commit* and thereby *choose* to being responsible for a task that has to be accomplished, it not only empowers us, but also ensures that others can rally around us and contribute to the desired goal. Besides, if during the process of getting the task done you were to encounter some hurdles or obstacles, you would creatively determine ways to tide over the setback, rather than lapse into a state of apportioning blame or seeking victimhood.

Commitment and taking responsibility is something that comes from *within* each one of us. It is a part of our interiority and has to do with what we wish to pursue. These choices are also exercised based on how we—as individuals—would like the world to perceive us. This choice is also the basis of what ancient Indian texts refer to as one's 'dharma'.

We need to add, however, that making choices that yield beneficial outcomes for an individual can be *learned*. A key ingredient of this learning process is depending on factors that are in one's control: also called the 'I Factors'. Those who are not accountable rely on the 'They Factors': things or actions that—they think—others have to do! If those actions by others—people or agencies such as the government, the head of your department, your professor, your spouse or anyone else for that matter—do not get done, or the desired situations do not 'arise', people who focus on the 'they factors' end up doing nothing and feeling powerless and miserable.

We know from experience that human beings reflect great diversity in their temperaments and what may be called their 'nature'. Therefore, we approach life's myriad interactions and experiences in very different ways. Yet, a choice to be accountable, and focusing on the things one can do, is a quality that gets stronger with practice.

Like so many other habits, the more we make the choice of being accountable, the better we get at it.

Accountability Transforms Circumstances

Exercising the choice of being accountable and deciding to rely on the factors in one's control can dramatically alter one's approach to life's myriad situations for the better.

Many of you might wonder how can a simple change of committing to be accountable—which is really a change you are making 'within yourself'—make a difference to the circumstances on the 'outside'?

Anyone would have this doubt. The beauty is that your inner filters make a big difference to the way your brain perceives outside stimuli (see the Section on 'Thinking, Feeling and Behaving' where this point has been addressed in detail). So when you make a choice to take ownership of and be responsible for dealing with any situation that you might experience (which is what being accountable is, after all), your whole being *responds* very differently than if you were to you think that you are at the mercy of circumstances.

Dr Richard Alpert, a Stanford PhD in Psychology and later a professor at Harvard, came to India in the 1960s and the 1970s and learned meditation from his Indian Guru, Neem Karoli Baba. He acquired the name of Ram Dass and wrote a powerful book entitled *Remember, Be Here Now*. One of his favourite stories related to prisoners, whom he had worked with. He would tell the inmates of 'solitary confinement' that they should 'think' that they are in a monastery because in monasteries, too, monks live in a cell, are given food at regular hours and have to spend time by themselves (in solitude). He would then teach them to meditate and depend entirely on their own interiority to feel peaceful. The results, which he documented, included making the inmates more peaceful (less violent), more productive and generally useful in the facility.

Helping to change the inner perspective of prisoners, with beneficial outcomes, is a great example. It reinforces the fact that becoming accountable can help each one of us, irrespective of the circumstances that we might find ourselves in. Placing attention on factors that one can influence, change or modify—including the way one looks at one's condition—is a potent transformative tool.

This does not mean that factors beyond you—events or situations beyond your control—will not play a role. Of course they will! But with you wilfully focusing on what you can do, now, rather than allowing the circumstances to overwhelm you, opens up a whole new set of possibilities.

That is why even a situation that could ordinarily 'drive you nuts' could become one where you are in complete command of your emotions. Instead of feeling that you are being driven to lunacy by people or by certain conditions, you will now focus on how you can modify whatever is changeable. This inner change will make for a different outcome and response—as well as a healthier, happier emotional state—than before.

The Tale of Two Managers

There are two colleagues—Mr A and Mr B—both of whom are working at a number of marinas in a mid-sized coastal city in the southeast of the USA. Both 'A' and 'B' are managers and report to the same boss: the department head of the firm they all work for. The company is a manufacturer of safety devices and equipment used by large private boats, and they also provide security services to their well-heeled clients.

'A' and 'B' are together responsible for securing the safety of their client's yachts at various marinas in the city, on the edge of the Atlantic Ocean.

The two colleagues work independently. 'A' is responsible for ensuring that the marinas in the company's care are well guarded and fully deployed with their company's safety equipment, so as not to allow intruders in.

'B' ensures that each yacht or boat is parked at the marina only after it has followed the company's documented protocols for the security equipment installed inside each yacht. This is to prevent its theft as well as pilferage of whatever valuable items it might have on board.

On one occasion a yacht is robbed. The client, a rich tycoon, threatens to not use the company's equipment and the company-monitored marina ever again if the company does not recover all the stolen items and pays him handsomely by way of damages. This is clearly a serious demand. The matter is quickly escalated to the level of the firm's CEO.

The CEO of the company calls the two colleagues over and gives them a serious 'tongue lashing' for their combined lapse. He finally threatens them by saying that if the stolen goods are not found within a certain time frame, then he would deduct the damages payable to the rich client from their salaries and their annual bonuses, apart from demoting or firing them! All this, even if the insurance company would cover the damages!

'A' has learned to be accountable. 'B', on the other hand, does not practise being accountable. Though they were both 'grilled over hot coals', their responses are completely different.

'A' looks at the sequence of events up to the time when the theft was discovered. He endeavours to recreate the conditions when his team went about its work, trying to identify the flaws or errors that might have contributed to the lapses and led to the theft.

'B' on the other hand just begins to blame 'A' and his team. He is agitated by the fact that he has been reprimanded by the CEO

and might even lose his earnings and possibly his job. He is reacting to the same situation with anguish and despair. Since being
reprimanded, he has not stopped whining:

> I did my job the way I do it every day. My team followed all the steps,
> as always, to secure the yachts. A and his team *must have* missed out
> on something. Someone must have intruded on account of the errors
> made by him and his team. It might even be an inside job....

The outcome is predictable. Instead of 'A' and 'B' working together
to figure out the deficiencies in the overall system, 'B' sulks and
is no longer willing to apply his mental resources to analyse a
difficult situation with the intention of solving it collaboratively
with 'A'.

'A', however, is far more focused despite the pressures that he
also feels within himself. He looks at what he could have done differently and what changes his team and he can make in their
approach to security for the future. His emotional state is more
relaxed, since he appreciates that an error has occurred and while it
might result in a loss of earnings and prestige for him personally, it
is not the end of the world. Besides, he views it as a situation where
he *chooses* to use his creative and other faculties to prevent a recurrence of similar undesirable situations again.

The difference between 'A' and 'B', therefore, lies only in their
attitude and their individual choices. 'A' is centred in himself and
is *accountable* and *action oriented*. He feels a burst of renewed energy
because of his using the event (i.e., the theft) to creatively diagnose
the root causes of the situation and prevent their recurrence.

On the other hand, 'B' is sulking and alienating himself from
others by blaming them, and then getting into a shell. He also
refuses to engage with the others in the team in a constructive manner, because he is upset and hence disinclined.

'B' is quite likely to *feel* that his boss and 'A' together conspired
to make his life miserable. The tragedy is that each time 'B' gets into
the groove of blaming others and cursing his luck for the misery
that fate and others are piling upon him, he actually feels more
like a 'victim of circumstances' and is, therefore, all the more
miserable.

Can you think of the outcome of this tale? Spend a little time reflecting on the outcome that you have thought of. Why is your outcome likely? What could 'A' or 'B' have done differently?

Choosing Your Focus

The tale of the Chinese farmer in the Middle Ages provides a perceptive view of life's events.

This farmer had a beautiful riding horse that was much admired for its grace and speed. One day the horse ran away. The neighbours came to commiserate with the farmer over his terrible loss. The farmer said, 'Maybe it is not bad fortune.' The neighbours went away shaking their heads in utter disbelief at the man's foolishness.

A month later, the horse came home—this time bringing with her a number of other beautiful wild horses. The neighbours became excited at the farmer's good fortune. Such lovely strong horses! The farmer said, 'Maybe it is not such good fortune.'

The farmer's son was thrown off while trying to ride one of the wild horses. He broke his leg. All the neighbours were very distressed. 'Such bad luck!' they said. The farmer said, 'Maybe it is not so bad.'

A war came and the king's soldiers rounded every able-bodied man for conscription and being sent into battle. Only the farmer's son, because he had a broken leg, was not taken. The neighbours congratulated the farmer. 'Maybe it is not so good.' said the farmer.

Whenever you encounter a situation, you will—with a little practice—realize that the things that constitute the occurrence as a whole have two main features. There are those aspects that are completely random and cannot be controlled or mitigated by prior planning or actions on your part. The other aspect concerns your reactions to the event and the subsequent outcome of the situation itself.

As a human being, any event or situation can only yield two outcomes *within* yourself: you can either feel depressed or unhappy with what has happened or you can feel elated and joyful. That is what the Chinese farmer's story illustrates beautifully: Out of habit people *presume* that some events are 'good' while others are 'bad'.

They forget that events are neutral and our state of mind is a consequence of the choices we make.

It helps to be focused on the right view.

Starting with the Right Outcomes

Two Zen monks were given two identical metal bowls to clean by their master. Both the bowls were dark and discoloured from years of use.

One of the monks went to the edge of the river and using clay and fine gravel from the bank scoured the bowl till it shone in the Sun. Still not satisfied with the look of the bowl, the monk got some acid and used it to remove all the blemishes, till he was satisfied that the bowl had been cleaned perfectly.

The other monk, however, just took a moist cloth and wiped his bowl clean with a few gentle swipes.

When the monks returned to their master, he poured water into them both. The bowl that was sparkling had sprung a leak and couldn't hold water. The other bowl was fine.

Very often we all behave like the monk that shone his bowl to perfection. We forget the real *outcomes* that we wish to achieve, getting distracted by secondary goals or events along the way.

Some distractions are natural. There are so many more variables that make up life that to think that one can control or plan for them all is sheer folly. Many outcomes, despite our efforts, may not be as we wish.

A person gets sick. This is not unusual. Focusing on the right outcome, the 'I' factors in this situation would include how one 'chooses to respond' to the ailment.

Instead of blaming one's luck, the pathogens or one's genes, it would help if one were to focus on achieving good health and taking all steps (prevention, hygiene, medication, meditation and the right blend of food and exercise) needed for a rapid restoration of health or the most comfortable state. That would keep the mind at rest and ensure that one does not drain one's emotional energy blaming one's body or some organ within.

By being accountable and focusing on the right outcomes, as well as on the factors in our control, any situation can be handled appropriately. Simultaneously, we would be keeping ourselves emotionally steady and focused on the right actions.

As an accountable person, any and all the actions on our part—in whatever situation—may or may not alter the triggering behaviour of the other party or change the circumstances that we experience. This is true for all our myriad interactions and experiences. What does happen, however, is that we remain sufficiently focused to take action on those factors that are in our control.

This in itself is a noteworthy achievement and contributes substantially to being poised and relaxed at all times.

Accountability and Teamwork

The secret of individual accountability is very aptly rendered in the 'Serenity Prayer'.

God, grant me the serenity to accept the things I cannot change,

The courage to change the things I can,

And the wisdom to know the difference.

This prayer was originally written by the American theologian Reinhold Niebuhr, sometime in the mid-1940s, and beautifully helps us to focus on the things that are truly in our control.

The performance of excellent teams is obviously a function of the well-coordinated efforts of all those comprising the team. This also implies that everyone would have to hold themselves and one another responsible and accountable for the work that has been entrusted to them as a part of the team's goals. This is where individual commitment and accountability play a part.

Let us assume that some members of a team are not sufficiently committed to the outcomes that their group is pursuing. Even in this case there would be many levers—in one's control as an individual team player—that one could work upon to ameliorate or improve the situation. For instance, as team members we could convene a meeting to discuss the performance of the team as well as that of individual members. If the team reports to a supervisor, that person could be alerted. Even a team meeting could be called, where the laggards are given feedback—in a non-threatening way—on how their actions are impacting the group. Besides, we could even suggest that someone within the team, with the requisite skills, could coach the members whose performance is not up to the mark.

This is just an indicative list of the possibilities, but it demonstrates that even when the performance of a larger group is interlinked with that of individuals, one does not have to relinquish 'charge' of whatever factors are within one's control, even as one works for the accomplishment of the group goals. This accountability orientation—present even in a few people—can make a big difference to the group's overall performance and is likely to result in the team's output exceeding expectations.

In the remote case where the results achieved by the group do not reach the predetermined expectations, the fact that *individual efforts* were made to rectify the output, even as the team was going about its business, would greatly enhance the satisfaction within the group. Collectively, team harmony would improve and the team would be better prepared for the next challenge.

Being accountable is not without its visible benefits as well!

(E) Health and Well-being

Health is Real Wealth

There is no better foundation for a lifetime of joy and fulfilment than being in a state of good physical and mental health. It is not for nothing that wise people, who have lived long lives, continue to remind us that 'health is the real wealth!'

When we are young we do not always realize that to lead a life that is healthy and which ensures our physical and emotional well-being for long years requires some actions on our part. Good health and long-term well-being are not just dependent on one's genes. Genes play a part, but right choices can still be made. There is much in one's own hands that can make a significant, positive difference to how our bodies and minds behave.

What is needed is that we first become *aware* of what makes our bodies and our minds work diligently; then we can strengthen those aspects of our selves that contribute to health and well-being.

Body, Mind and the Animating Spirit

The human body with all its organs, extraordinary capabilities and characteristics has a finite lifespan. This period, recorded in years, is the time between when we were born and when we drop our bodies. *Awareness* of this reality is a very important part of the process of learning to live a joyful and fulfilling life even as we navigate the maze.

If our bodies suffer pain or discomfort, it is we—alone and without any of our loved ones or relatives—who will have to bear the burden of dealing with the pain. Even if there is discomfort or the body 'lacks ease'—or is in a state of 'disease'—the burden of dealing with the resultant suffering rests squarely on the one who is experiencing it. At a time when the body–mind is in pain in some way, nobody can bring relief. The only source of succour is to bring one's own body and mind back into a healthy, relaxed state.

Often the composite term 'bodymind' is used to refer to the visible and the invisible parts of our personality, both of which play a critical role in the maintenance of our overall health and longevity. As we have mentioned in earlier sections of this chapter, our bodies and minds do function collectively and one impacts the other in many complex ways. Hence, the use of this conjoined term. So in reality, any endeavour to ensure lasting well-being needs to focus on our body–mind, or simply our 'bodymind'.

One critical key to health and well-being is awareness—awareness of our bodies, its functions, our minds and our emotions. *Awareness* is thus a process where one is conscious of and able to *watch* one's body and *know* the functioning of one's mind and one's relationship with one's surroundings. Awareness helps to reveal that one's consciousness is separate and located in a space that is separate from the aggregates that we might consider to be a part of our body–minds.

Another key to health requires one to be very watchful and alert about what gives the body ease and comfort. We have to *know* that our body–mind is animated by a 'life force' or a 'spirit' that plays a vital role in the way our body functions. We need to appreciate that the 'life force' is responsible for most of the amazing qualities of our body–mind. Our endeavour, therefore, has to be to allow for this spirit to flow freely through our bodies and to enable its intrinsic, life-supporting qualities to nurture every cell, every tissue and every small or large organ in our complex body–minds.

This life-animating force works best when the mind is calm, one's emotions are peaceful and the body is at ease. We do not use the word 'ease' to reflect passivity or inaction; instead, being 'at ease' implies being in a state of 'easiness' where everything that you might be doing is 'flowing' out of you, without any stress or strain. In fact, it is only when the body, mind, emotions and the animating spirit are in a 'dynamic harmony' that a discernible sense of well-being and health pervade.

There is also a physiological reason for the life force to perform flawlessly, when our minds are still and not full of 'external noise' or inner chatter. Our brains need large quantities of oxygen to perform their thinking and coordinating functions within the body. When the mind is still, the oxygen requirements are reduced and the spare oxygen is then used by the next big user of that element in our bodies—our bone marrow. Our bone marrow is the factory for producing red and white blood cells, apart from a host of other lymphocytes that contribute to the body's immune system and well-being.

A still mind, therefore, contributes to the generation of healthier and more profuse red and white blood cells, which boost stamina and immunity. Similar benefits are obtained from exercise, where the body and the exerted tissues receive more oxygen and, hence, develop improved capabilities as a result.

Being aware of our body and mind and their functioning is the first step to gain mastery over them. We are not our minds or bodies. They are our instruments to do as *we choose*. Being aware of this prevents our enslavement to the habitual, and often erroneous, workings of our minds or the cravings of our bodies.

A Recipe for Health and Well-being

Enabling the animating life spirit to flow freely through our body–minds at all times, ensuring a peaceful and aligned interiority, is the 'secret sauce' for lasting good health and well-being. Clearly, whatever can become an obstruction or an impediment to the easy functioning of the heart (loosely, the 'seat of the animating spirit') has to be discarded or eliminated from our experiences.

Regulated and restful sleep for six to eight hours a day is recommended. The food choices we make have to have a healthy mix of proteins, grains, pulses and greens. Unhealthy processed foods, containing preservatives, sugars and chemicals, need to be avoided. We can make a beginning by ensuring that we eat the right foods. We can focus on consuming those foods that are nutritious and provide a balance of the essential elements and vitamins that are needed to keep us healthy.

Apart from healthy food and adequate sleep, exercise and immersing ourselves in enjoyable activities—throughout our lives—are equally essential. Choosing to care about these important aspects of well-being is entirely in our own hands.

We also need to ensure that we do not consciously ingest toxins into our system—inappropriate foods, drinks or chemicals that may be imbided. Many are known to have a deleterious effect on our body–minds, and while it is socially acceptable in many cultures to ingest such 'foods, drugs and drink', one has to determine one's own limits. Going beyond one's limit could impair one's functioning and be dangerous.

We need to minimize and ultimately eliminate the ingestion of alcohol, narcotics, nicotine, tobacco or any of the psychedelic chemicals that are being used to give people a temporary 'rush' or a 'high'.

We often take in such chemicals with a lack of awareness and because we are often seduced by those who tell us that the toxins can help us to 'fit into the group', 'work harder and smarter' or become 'successful'. There can be no lasting well-being if we pump in poisons into our systems. Besides, the myriad consequences that follow will be for each one of us to bear alone. Toxins are especially harmful to the mind and adversely impact the serene flow of the life-giving spirit through our body–minds.

To exercise regularly, we can join a gym, participate in dancing, Zumba, Tai-chi, spinning, yoga, Pilates, stretching or any other form that is compatible with our constitution and with our liking. The focus is to ensure body flexibility, agility, strength, endurance and balance. Increased stamina with improved cardio-vascular health are beneficial outcomes of the right kinds of exercises.

Lifelong health and well-being are assured if—within the broad parameters of your genetic make-up and the salutary role of providence—one maintains consistency and regularity in discipline. Eating right and exercising regularly are both essential all through one's life. These cannot be done for a few weeks and then dropped. Being in silence for prolonged periods, minimizing the stimuli that your senses receive (switching off the TV, the iPad, smartphone and removing the headphones!) and developing one's awareness through appropriate meditative practices are also essential for a lifetime of health and well-being. The sooner we get into a regimen for the well-being of our body–minds, the better.

This calls for each one of us to demonstrate eagerness, a determination and a commitment to living a life of good health and wellness. Working regularly, thereafter, to a time-bound plan to achieve our essential and beneficial goals is the next step. Then holding on to the gains, for the rest of one's life, is the final element.

It is said that people who have learned to master themselves can master the world. As the great artist, philosopher, inventor and humanist Leonardo da Vinci said:

> You will never have a greater or lesser dominion than that over yourself...the height of a man's success is gauged by his self-mastery; the depth of his failure by his self-abandonment. ...And this law is the expression of eternal justice. He who cannot establish dominion over himself will have no dominion over others.

SIMPLE STARTING STRATEGIES

Self-mastery

✓ Dwell on and internalize this important idea: we have the power to choose how we may respond to any situation.

✓ Understand how negative emotions well up when we allow stimuli to hijack our rational thinking processes.

✓ Understand the beliefs that you have about things that are important to you by examining your self-talk.

✓ Identify those beliefs that are limiting your evolution to your higher self.

✓ Work on dumping self-limiting beliefs.

✓ Practice mindfulness all the time.

✓ Know that you are life's child and unique in this infinite cosmos. There is none akin to you. Your uniqueness requires you to be your own master.

✓ Take responsibility for your life by being accountable.

✓ Focus on the 'I Factors' when you encounter a situation

✓ Let the locus of control be within you.

✓ Live life focusing on the things that are truly valuable. Strive for balance in life.

✓ Let your natural state of joy, peace of mind, health and well-being manifest through the right thoughts and right actions.

✓ Use your body well. Take care of it. It is your instrument to use to reach your highest potential.

(F) Queries and Responses for Chapter 1

Is charisma a 'gift of god' or can one acquire it?
In the strictest of definitions, 'charisma' is defined as a divinely conferred gift or power. It is our view, however, that all of us have the animating life spirit flowing through us, and hence, there is no person, who is not touched by the divine at all times! So from that perspective, anyone and everyone can be charismatic!

If you understand charisma as the sum of all those personal qualities that give a person influence or authority over a large number of people, then there is no doubt that the way a person looks and behaves will play a role. Some of these attributes are given by nature. But other aspects of interactional excellence, and the way one speaks, behaves and grooms one self, can all be learned. Thereby, anyone can enhance what we could refer to as their 'grace factor' or GF.

Removing one's behavioural rough edges and being courteous, sensitive and respectful to all would add to one's GF. Learning the art of presenting one's ideas effectively with impact as well as with the appropriate protocol would also contribute to this. Finally, being an action-oriented, accountable individual would also work wonders on others viewing you as charismatic.

I have a large 'following' of friends and family, who I think over-estimate my capabilities. Is this a problem?
There is never a problem in having a 'fan' following of friends and family. There must be some good qualities, wholesome interactional abilities and behavioural traits that you possess, which endears you to people. If people acknowledge and appreciate your gifts, and are willing to be guided and led by you, that is indeed good news!

The fact that you think your following 'overestimates' your qualities needs to be explored further. It is often true that intimate friends and those who are fond of you can be overenthusiastic in praising you and might have difficulty seeing your flaws. You need to be aware of this and discount what your cheering friends tell you. In fact, in the tale 'The Emperor's New Clothes' a lack of awareness on part of the emperor, and his being surrounded by a servile and fawning set of courtiers, really made the poor king think that he was wearing the world's finest clothes of spun gold when in reality he was stark naked!

From a perspective of your self-esteem, the bigger point is whether you will still feel 'good' and 'comfortable' without the following of an adulatory set of people. If the answer is, 'no', or 'maybe not', then it is worthwhile to go through the Section on 'Self-esteem and Self-worth' of this chapter without any further delay!

I was not selected for any corporate job during campus placements, even though everyone thought that getting a job would be a 'piece of cake' for me. What do you think went wrong?
Nothing went wrong. You and your friends thought that you had all the skills and the smarts to get a job. But the companies that did come for placement, and for the kind of job openings that they were keen to fill, may not have seen evidence of the skills, the experience or the aptitude in you that they were looking for.

There is a remote chance that the adulatory feedback from your friends did make you complacent and you did not prepare for the selection process adequately. The laxity in preparation and the overconfidence during the interviews may have ticked off the selectors!

There are a number of criteria that determine who gets a job and who doesn't. It is often a question of the selectors looking for the 'best fit' between the attributes they are seeking and those available in the candidates they assess. Not getting a certain job is an indication that your skill set did not offer the best fit. This is fine, because your unique blend of skills and experience will ensure a good fit in some other job or vocation.

There is also an element of subjectivity that can come into play during a selection interview. Therefore, treating the decision of such a panel as the 'end of the road' for you is improper and demonstrates that you are making a wrong choice (see the first and second sections of the chapter).

How would I know if I have taken a path which will help me grow and be happy, even though it might be so different from what I might ever have done before?
You would have come across many people who took dramatic turns in their lives/careers just to follow their dreams. Following your

dream is essentially a process of trusting your interiority, and *knowing* that your dream is uniquely yours to follow. You know that if you take the road that is meant for you, you will be enthused and will experience peace and joy.

The answer to your question is that you would know you are on the 'right' path if you feel lighter, less stressed and more energetic when you decide to take the path. This sense of 'feeling good' inside is the surest sign. Doing something different but which is satisfying is a wonderful way to achieve your full potential!

When you have a doubt about which fork in the road you need to take, practice silence and listen to your inner voice for guidance.

It is often said that one must keep one's personal thoughts at home while going to work. But we have only one mind, so is this possible at all?

Our minds have enormous power and potential. The speed at which we process terabytes of information—received through our senses alone—exceeds that of some of the world's fastest computers!

Our minds are the place where all our thoughts emerge and all our memories reside. If we are not mindful of how the mind throws up thoughts, we are very likely to be swayed by them and carried far away from the present moment.

Keeping one's personal thoughts at home, even as you are at work, is therefore not possible. If you go to work, your mind goes with you! Whatever is in the mind will all be there as well.

However, the reason why the suggestion is given is to remind you that if you wish to be effective at work, you will have to be wholly present at work and not be 'daydreaming' or 'wandering' with any extraneous thoughts that might be bubbling up in your mind. It is quite normal to suddenly think of something that might need your attention at home, after work. You could jot down that point in a pocket diary (keeping which is a good habit to cultivate) and attend to it when you are home. This will take a load off your thinking mind and help you to come back to the present moment, and give your 100% attention to work.

Looking around, one notices a competitive 'rat race' in which everyone seems engrossed. Where do all these people want to go? Each and every person in the world is pursuing a set of goals or a bunch of desires. Some are eagerly 'going after things' to accomplish. This is the way we are.

A goal that drives someone to pursue it vigorously might not inspire or motivate another person. But all those who are following their dreams, or their life's purpose with zeal, might seem like they are running a race—a competitive endeavour to reach the top of some real or imagined pinnacle! This is just fine, since we are all unique and have our own preferences and choices. Hence pursuing our own dreams and goals is wonderful.

There is undoubtedly a need to balance the pursuit of one's dreams with the time taken to nurture one's spirit. Throughout this book, we remind ourselves that what is truly valuable in life is a gift from Existence. Finding the time to appreciate this, expressing gratitude for these blessings and nurturing that which Existence has abundantly offered are deeply enriching. Placing one's goals in the context of life's gifts helps to temper the competitive aspect of the 'rat race' and bring balance, harmony and joy into our lives.

Each of us has to determine our unique purpose and use one's talents and competencies to serve and add to the joy and well-being of all of life's creations. We are free to choose a path aligned with our calling.

If competition is not for you, so be it. Those who have chosen a journey that is competitive are entitled to the consequences of their choice and we can leave it at that.

Is being selfish today's bottom line?

Throughout human history, people from all cultures and nationalities have been on a continuum—where one end is altruism and the other selfishness. So it is not as if the pursuit of things for one's own self—often at the cost of the well-being of others—is something new or a factor of these times alone.

The bigger and more relevant question is: Where on the continuum do *you* wish to be? Being anywhere is a personal choice, but whatever you choose you have to be prepared to deal with the consequences of your choice. We are not suggesting that some choices are 'good' and the others are 'bad'. We accept and understand that the miracle of life requires the whole continuum to be populated.

Here are a few philosophical insights that might help you make a choice that is best for you:

1. Fruits on trees that are abundantly laden can never be eaten by the trees 'themselves'. The same holds true for the ears of corn that cannot feed the stalks they are on.
2. Take our nearest star, the Sun. This effulgent shining orb, that sustains life, gives its life force and energy to one and all—never being miserly or discriminating. What does the Sun expect in return?
3. The male lion, after vanquishing the dominant male of a pride of lionesses, immediately sets out to kill the little cubs that have been sired by the old lion. Only when all the cubs are dead, and out of the way, will the new victor mate the same lionesses to ensure that his genes alone spread through future generations.

So nature has some wonderful and simple 'sermons' to offer us humans. All parts of the continuum need to be populated and you can choose where you wish to be. Being helpful or not is a choice one makes. Whatever consequences this orientation bears, these are for us to face and accept. Nobody is forcing you to be helpful. It *could* be a source of joy and peace for your heart and soul. But if you choose to be on some part of the continuum to appease and please *others*, then this choice too needs to be revisited and questioned.

I always wish to help others at work and am known to be helpful. But I never receive help from my colleagues. Should I stop being helpful?
Please take a minute to go over our response to the above question about 'selfishness'.

As we suggest, being a certain way is a choice you have to make. However, if you are being helpful at work because you are trying to 'look good' in the eyes of your superior, or are trying to please your team mates, then you may need to revisit your 'helpful' orientation.

The other point concerns working as a member of a team. If you end up being given all the work that is assigned to the team and have to spend long hours at work while the others can leave on time, there is an imbalance that needs to be corrected. You would need to assertively convey to your team members that the inequitable distribution of work is something that you do not appreciate. You would have to get the team to work on a solution together, which keeps you from being overloaded while the others also contribute to accomplish the team's tasks.

As for stopping being helpful, look at it this way: Would not being helpful define you as a person better? Would you feel happier? If the answer to these questions is 'yes', then you can make a choice accordingly. Just remember that the backwash of your choices and actions would be for you to bear.

I do not have the courage to refuse taking on an assignment entrusted to me by my superior, which I know I do not have the competence to accomplish. Yet, having said 'yes' to the boss, how do I cope with this situation?

Saying 'yes', when you should actually be saying 'no', is a cause for stress in many people. Many people carry this erroneous assumption in their minds that prompts self-talk of this kind:

'If I acknowledge my lack of sufficient knowledge about this matter or convey that I cannot do it, I will be insulted or ridiculed by all.'

Many Oriental cultures—including that of India—place great emphasis on a person not 'losing face'. Hence, many of our behaviours are driven by the kind of self-talk mentioned earlier as well as a deep urge for us to 'save face' at all times. Saying 'no' therefore becomes difficult. However, the ability to refuse something, politely and firmly, is a fundamental skill for one's long-term interpersonal well-being and for not being weighed down under needless stress (this might be a good time to read Chapter 2).

To deal with the situation that you have described, it is recommended that you deal with the matter with truthfulness and honesty. You can approach your boss when he or she is alone and in an assertive and direct fashion state your inability to do the assignment. Explain to him or her why you think you are not the best person for that task. This needs to be done as soon as possible and definitely well before the boss and others in your team *think* that you are on 'top of the assignment'. The more you delay this honest and direct communication with your superior, the tougher it will get for you and the more anxious you are likely to feel.

In all probability, your senior will be appreciative of your honesty and will assist you with additional resources, or the guidance of experts, so that the task is accomplished as expected.

Everyone in my friends' circle tries to demotivate me. They say that I'm useless and can't do anything worthwhile. Even if I do my work well, someone else will take the credit. Will this be my fate in an industry that I might join? Will such behaviour be demonstrated even by those in whom I trust?

You are making an assumption that what you are experiencing within your friends' circle today, will repeat when you start working in some organization.

It might be helpful to examine why your friends speak harshly to you. Have you given them cues through your verbal or nonverbal communications that you are lacking in something? Or have you ever shared that there are some things that you do not enjoy? Friends do sometimes 'latch on' to the very things that we have told them, so it might be a good idea to be judicious with what information you share with whom.

Moving to a newer setting gives you a tremendous opportunity to start afresh. Share information appropriately with the right people. Develop your confidence and learn to be assertive.

Furthermore, your confidence and faith in your abilities will help you achieve your goals and deliver results. Let the experiences that you had with your friends be left behind and start your assignment within your preferred industry with renewed zeal.

It may happen that someone at your workplace may still want to take credit for your accomplishments. In such situations, you will have to be assertive and directly address the issue with the person involved. Using 'I phrases' is the right way to convey your feelings directly, and that, too, without getting impolite or angry.

You may still not be able to convince your colleagues that they have taken credit for something that you have done. Nonetheless, because you expressed your feelings about their behaviour, you will feel good about having spoken up. If not, you can report your colleague's behaviour to your supervisor. However, keep in mind that in organizations it is helpful to choose your battles wisely. If after repeated efforts you still see no changes to rectify the error, you may decide to let this event/situation pass and close the chapter. The attitude, 'don't sweat the small stuff—and it is all small stuff' can be helpful.

2

Interactional Excellence

Interactions Are Enriching

A sage in the mountains has chosen to stay away from the crowds of the plains and live his life in a 'silo'. That invariably breeds 'isolation'. But it is a choice that has been made and bearing the consequences of that decision appeal to the sage. Most of us are either not drawn to such choices or we prefer different lifestyles, especially the kind where we are in the midst of people and interactions.

Our lives are, therefore, full of interactions which we have with people and with other living beings. Human life benefits from communications that are positive and joyful. Individuals and groups require engagement with others to live enriched, fulfilled and happy lives. Studies from around the world, including a specific Harvard University study which has run continuously since 1938, confirm that managing conflicts appropriately, engaging in warm and friendly social interactions and the forging of lasting bonds—such as through marriage or kinship within a family and with close friends—contribute the most to physical and emotional health, longevity and to the overall quality of life that one leads.

Yet within interactions, the lack of appropriate interpersonal skills contributes to a great deal of emotional pain, anger, frustration, reduced well-being, hurt and heartache. So, on the one hand, we 'need' to interact and develop relationships with others, and on the other, because of lack of awareness, sensitivity and skills of interacting appropriately, we end up with negative emotions and feelings. This can be confusing and unsettling. Many a time, we might choose to get into a 'shell', become a loner, a recluse and avoid interacting.

So what is the pain point and what can be done about it? The 'problem'—if that term can be used—lies in the fact that we have either not learned or practised the skills of effective communication enough. Communicating and using our abilities to connect with people, share our views, forge friendships, solve issues, take decisions, negotiate and deal with conflicts is a critical skill set. These skills are greatly impacted, both positively and negatively, by our ability to manage our attitudes, beliefs, emotions and situations.

The usual response of blaming the 'other' for a communication breakdown does not work. Proactively recognizing the issue, taking responsibility and doing what is appropriate in the moment will help in mending the situation and saving the relationship. The process of learning the required skills for interpersonal effectiveness, therefore, has to go hand-in-hand with a conscious endeavour to attain self-mastery. It is an art that can be developed through diligence and practice, like any other skill. The benefits far outweigh the effort.

One of the critical skills of developing and then mastering interactional excellence remains 'communication', which is a term that we hear being used all the time—from those in school management to corporate leadership, politicians to university students, restaurant owners to export houses and medicare professionals to patient caregivers.

We have, in the following sections, demystified the term and highlighted its relevance besides sharing methods that help in enhancing this ability. Existence has truly blessed us humans with this amazing and essential human capability.

(A) Communication and Building Relationships

Communication Basics

'Communication', a word that we have heard a 'zillion' times, means diverse things to diverse people. Irrespective of the meaning that we may assign to this word, we can never doubt its importance in our day-to-day lives.

From the moment babies are born, and even before they have learnt to vocalize and speak, they start communicating with people around. Those attending to infants—the parents, grandparents, visitors and nannies—are soon able to interpret what the newborn is trying to convey.

The communication process, in its simplest form, involves a speaker/sender, a receiver, a message and a medium or the channel used. What completes the loop is the feedback from the one who is listening or reading the message to the sender.

As we grow in years, we become skilled at the wonderful ability to use appropriate words and phrases to convey our ideas, thoughts, feelings and emotions. We get better and better at this as we understand the nuances of the language we are using and the subtle differences between words. We also realize that communicating through speech requires us to use not just our vocal chords to verbalize what we are trying to convey but our bodies to confirm and convey the same message as well. The non-verbal part of communication is as important as the verbal.

There is no doubt that we all need to communicate. We do not use the vehicle of communication only to inform or instruct. There are several other equally important reasons for delving into the world of words and symbols. On a regular basis, we plan, manage, negotiate, supervise and organize ourselves as well as resources and other people to achieve desirable results. The success of all these activities hinges on effective communication. Proper and effective communication is integral to situations where specific goals are being achieved.

Unlike the rest of the animal world, where an animal that is exposed to a perceived threatening situation either 'fights' or takes 'flight', the evolved *Homo sapiens* have the unique ability of demonstrating verbal fluency and that broadens the repertoire of responses available to us. This broadened ability to use language to deal with threatening and diverse situations, with the right kind of messaging, enables us to have social interactions that can be friendly, supportive of one another and can—if done right—bring great joy and satisfaction.

Humans are social beings, and our lives are greatly enriched through interactions and bonding with others. Love is expressed, feelings are made known and caring is demonstrated through a reliance on the many varied nuances of communication. Hence, communication that is light-hearted, free-flowing, without an agenda, humorous and fun, adds great value to human interactions (as well as interactions with pets!) and makes life a delight to live!

Understanding the nuts and bolts of the process of communicating well is, therefore, worth the investment. It is completely doable to master this ability.

The Benefits, Please!

There is a party at home. Besides extended family, Ritesh, a young adult, is also attending it. He stays in a separate apartment. After the guests leave, his mother Karuna offers to pack some food for him.

Karuna : 'Hey, I am going to pack some food for you to take along. Just wait, till I get the carry box.'

Ritesh : 'Please don't, Ma. I will have to dump the food into the garbage bin.'

Karuna : 'Why, dear?'

Ritesh : 'I have enough cooked food in my fridge. And I will have no other option but to trash it.'

The emotions that Karuna experienced on hearing Ritesh's response ranged from sadness to feeling hurt and disrespected. From then on, after every party or family get together, Ritesh would get none of the goodies while the others did!

There might have been some truth in the fact that Ritesh had enough food lying around at his place. But the way it was communicated left a bitter aftertaste.

Often we feel that we have been misunderstood. The easy way out of an unpleasant interactional situation—of course—is to put the responsibility and the blame on the other party. Yes, at times, the other party comes with its own set of 'barriers to communication' as well as 'emotional baggage' that aggravates circumstances and makes the possibility of dialogue even more remote.

If the intention is to have a harmonious relationship or at least a decent conversation, then dealing with the 'barriers' to the process, including any 'baggage' that might be lurking in the minds of either of the parties, is absolutely essential. For a successful interaction, both parties are equally accountable. As the former Chairman and CEO of Intel, Andrew 'Andy' Grove would say:

> How well we communicate is determined not by how well we say things, but how well we are understood.

If we are aware about the benefits that accrue from successful communications, surely we would like to invest time and effort into it. A few of the benefits deserve a special mention:

1. Building rapport and relationships
2. Problem-solving with inclusive decision-making and consensus
3. Team work and group effectiveness
4. Resolution of misunderstandings and conflicts
5. Superior and joyful interactions

When individuals and groups *make a choice* to have open and transparent communications and sharing, then over time, this commitment helps in developing and maintaining high levels of trust, loyalty and a reserve of warm feelings and goodwill. These feelings, in turn, make it easy to resolve issues and misunderstandings, as and when they surface. The level of confidence in putting forward one's thoughts, and conveying one's feelings and needs, gets greatly enhanced.

What more benefits would anyone want?

Excellence Starts with Effort

In the course of her many years of training and coaching individuals to make impactful presentations, Savita would hear a phrase repeatedly from many of her coachees: 'I am not a born communicator.'

We would like you to know that nobody is born with special skills. There is effort involved in becoming effective at communicating and interacting with others. It might seem like an uphill task to many, and as the process involves hard work, a number of people give up and make that hasty declaration that they are not naturally good at communication.

If you had a chance to question all those who might belong to a special club of excellent communicators, you will see evidence of hard work and preparation as the constant underpinning. They not only know what ingredients make for a successful communicating style and healthy relationships but also *put this knowledge into practice*, appropriately. A few other traits of these individuals are:

- Commitment to hone the ability of communicating effectively
- Eagerness to review their strengths objectively and openness to identifying areas of improvement
- Appreciation for the positive outcomes of learning and of using their new skills and abilities
- The belief that good communicators are not born but are products of continuous work and improvement.
- A willingness to learn from others by observing them and perfecting the attributes picked up.

The process of achieving interpersonal effectiveness and thereby forging lasting and harmonious relationships begins with *oneself*. The focus, like with many of the ideas contained in this book, therefore has to be on what you can do to achieve the outcomes that you desire. There is, however, one additional constituent that makes for the desired outcomes, especially when we are concerned about interpersonal effectiveness. That special 'potion' is one's *intention* and the clarity with which one wishes for a certain outcome to manifest in one's life.

The kind of feedback and responses we get, in the course of our interactions, will reinforce our faith in the need for developing and maintaining rapport and associations with our work partners as well as with personal contacts.

As stated earlier, the benefits are many and directly impact our business results, besides creating a relaxed and joyful ambience for work and leisure.

In a nutshell, the basic skills for interpersonal impact entail the following:

1. Putting across one's point of view in a clear, direct and focused manner.
2. Listening actively in an undistracted and complete manner. Listening to understand the other person's perspectives and opinions.
3. Giving and receiving feedback in a constructive way. The purpose being to remove or reduce any confusion or misunderstanding.
4. Being willing to acknowledge and address any conflicts that might arise.
5. Using dialogue and conversation to resolve the divergence and disagreement and to also arrive at a place where both parties feel heard, understood, comfortable and at ease.

Taking up the challenge of moving ahead by honing one's skills of communicating is completely doable and is in fact enjoyable too. There are no born communicators, really!

The Power of Intention

The valley of Kashmir was struck by conflict, strife, unrest and terror more than two decades ago. The minority community, fearing for their safety, had to suffer a mass exodus as they fled to safer regions outside the valley. In the span of just a few weeks, the frightened people left behind their homes, their ancestral properties, investments and valuables. Everyone affected was in deep anguish.

After a few years, when the violence showed no signs of abating, a few families decided to sell their properties and get what they could. Most were offered rock-bottom prices. Those who had no means went ahead with such distress sales.

One family had four children: two daughters and two sons, who along with their parents were stakeholders to the assets. The father entrusted one of the daughters, Suvidha—who was sharp and had the flair and interest in money matters—to handle the sale of the ancestral house and the documentation. The whole process of identifying the buyer, making the transfer papers and getting the proceeds of the sale were all handled by Suvidha.

Yet, at no point in the process did she think it necessary to either inform or consult the other siblings about the decisions that she was taking on behalf of the family.

How do you think Suvidha's relationship within her family shaped up after the transaction was done? Dwell on this for a while and make a list of points related to what Suvidha could have done to ensure that the family remained cohesive even as the sale of their house progressed to completion. Do you think Suvidha had the *intention* to share information, and get everybody on the same page, and keep the dealings transparent? Or was she too engrossed in the process to spend time sharing?

'Intention' is an internal, mental orientation within you that guides your behaviour in the direction in which you would like it to expand. What this means is that you have to first 'will' for something in your mind, before it can manifest outwardly. While having the right intention is imperative if one wishes to have excellent interpersonal relations, intention works its magic in just about every area of human endeavour!

It is very much a part of your interiority and, therefore, something that you alone can gauge. If you have the right intention about something, chances are that your thoughts and actions related to the intended outcome will also be aligned. Accordingly, you stand a far greater chance of reaching the outcome that you wished for in the first place. This is why it is said that there can never be an 'idle thought'.

Remember, we are designed for survival: So an evil intention may be disguised by unctuous words, but the non-verbal cues are far more difficult to disguise! More than that, the actions and behaviour say a lot about one's intention. In fact, as school children we heard the story of the 'mathematical horse' (the horse was called

Clever Hans; his story has been discussed in Chapter 1) which brought great fame to his owner, because any basic problem in math—conveyed to the horse—was always answered correctly with the right number of hoof taps on a board! Apparently the horse was so good with reading his master's body language that when the right number of taps had been made the master would relax and the horse would stop pounding!

If you have made it a habit to think that people will never find out what your true intentions are, you are wrong. Even young kids can make out what adults around them are conveying and how pure and clean their intent is.

Pure Intention

Our intentions arise from within our minds. If the intention springs from that part of the mind that identifies with the ego, the sense of 'I' that is driven by 'superiority' or 'differentness', the outcomes will not be positive. It will actually become an impediment to interacting wholesomely with others.

This is something that we would like to emphasize, because it is at the heart of living a life of peace, happiness and contentment. One cannot—and we are emphatic about this—ever live a life of joy and well-being, without one's intention emanating from the purest depths of one's consciousness. This is the same space where love and respect emanate and connect us to life itself. This connectedness promotes openness, fairness and justice, and makes us courageous.

Religions are meant to raise human consciousness to this higher level of realization. Yet more wars have been fought on the basis of religion! The intentions of the adversarial, warring groups throughout history—and it does not really matter which war or battle we are referring to—were all egocentric, driven by a desire to prove the superiority of one's faith or ideology over another. So dehumanizing can such ego-driven intentions be that one feels nothing as one inflicts pain on others, kills or maims in the name of the intended goal!

Therefore, in the context of interpersonal effectiveness, having and strengthening the *pure intention* of forging wholesome, positive, kind, loving, compassionate and lasting relations will make it happen. Together with a continuous endeavour to 'shine the light' on oneself, rather than blaming external situations: Being Accountable Positive intentions make the journey towards interpersonal effectiveness and harmonious relations easy, lasting, uplifting, nurturing and fruitful.

Content Aligns with Intent

Good communication starts with an A (for accuracy), a B (for brevity) and a C (for clarity of thinking and speaking).

The ABC of communication has to serve as the underlying foundation on which the rest of the preparation is built. For preparation, it is helpful to use the 5Ws (why, what, who, where and when) to guide us.

'Why' helps to define the objective of the interaction. Knowing why the communication or presentation is necessary helps to arrive at a clear idea as to what is intended to be accomplished. The purpose could vary from informing, persuading, guiding, entertaining, selling, motivating, inspiring, clarifying or counselling the other. Reminding ourselves of the purpose helps avoid unnecessary diversions and distractions.

'What' suggests what should be conveyed, based on the intention. Only when the purpose is clear can we decide on what the actual message and content ought to be.

While a bereaved family is experiencing grief, and the emotions that accompany the passing on of a loved one, people offer condolences to the family with phrases such as, 'We understand, how you feel. Please be strong for the rest of the family. We are always there for you.'

While the words may be appropriate, the intent and the sincerity with which the message is conveyed will influence how *exactly* the words sound and how they are received by the family.

'Who' pertains to the people, individuals or groups that will be hearing or receiving the message. This truly remains the most vital factor to be considered during the preparation for an impactful communication or conversation. Having thought through queries such as: who all are likely to be present? Is there clarity about the demographics (age, sex, race, nationality or religion, for instance) of the group? Are they aware what the discussion is about? Is the speaker or presenter aware of their expectations? Could they possibly have some hidden goals that might have to be addressed? All this information helps in deciding how the discussions can be planned and conducted.

A 'high-level' talk about nuclear fusion or fission is bound to be appreciated more by technically adept groups. Therefore, if the concepts have to be shared with a group of school-going children, the content will obviously have to be altered significantly and 'tweaked' to make it interesting and comprehensible to the youngsters.

'Where' is related to the place and the surroundings where the communication is to occur. The space and the setting play a silent, albeit a vital role on the quality of the conversation or presentation.

Imagine yourself in an alien and unsafe territory. Your capacity to share and put across a touchy or controversial point—even if factually impeccable—will be greatly stymied. You may fear that what you share may arouse anger or an adverse emotional response in the listeners. This might cramp your style as well as the content. That's why it is prudent not to be assertive with a mugger, late at night, in a dark alley. It is unwise, even if we think we have mastered this art of direct, forceful conversation.

We notice that individuals with authority will generally choose a place or seat that gives them an edge over others, in terms of a higher platform or a pedestal. This makes them feel more comfortable as they can 'look down' upon others. Or they may feel less nervous and, therefore, more worthy of speaking to an august gathering.

Many others perch themselves at a strategic position from where they can have a panoramic view of the gathering and watch the deliberations without being noticed. This is quite a smart thing to do. It is good to be aware of one's surroundings, the layout and positions taken by those around and then use that information to make oneself as comfortable within the setting as would allow for an impactful delivery of the message.

'When' pertains to the timing that has been chosen for the communication to happen. The timing of the communication is critical in ensuring that the message reaches the receiver with completeness and clarity. Many times, we experience an overwhelming need to speak and express ourselves. At such times, we often give little thought to the fact that the time may not be right or the occasion may be inappropriate for the message to be conveyed. Only after some damage is done, in terms of experiencing a negative emotion or a snapped relationship, do we remind ourselves that the timing was not appropriate.

A group of friends, all of whom are real *bum-chums*, are joined by another college mate. This friend is not known very well by all in the group. A rather 'expressive' pal decides to share some mischievous act of their group—something that the friends are not really proud of. In fact, the act could attract misdemeanour charges against the friends if the authorities were to find out. The friends are all horrified when—at the end of the conversation—the new entrant indicates that he works for college security cell. Sensitivity to the occasion, to the people, as well as the time during which a message is shared need to be kept in mind all the time and definitely during the actual interaction.

Of course, sometimes things just can't wait and delaying the news, information or a significant detail can be counterproductive too. Again, the right timing is of essence.

Rudyard Kipling (the British author, who was born in Mumbai in 1865 and died in London in 1936) wrote in a short limerick, 'I have six honest, serving men, who teach me all I know.' Five of those 'men' are the five Ws that have been introduced here. The sixth one, is H, 'How' to communicate. This represents the actual, real-time process.

Substance and Style

With the rise of cross-border and cross-country trade and business, and also with global mergers and acquisitions, people from different nationalities have to interact with each other to achieve results.

An American, Richard (R), is visiting India for the first time to meet with the business partner of his enterprise. He has a meeting with the patriarchal owner (O) of this medium-sized and well-known family-run business.

O: 'Today we will treat you to our special masala chai.'

R: 'I love trying out new things and foods. Please do serve it.'

Richard is offered home-made 'chai' with ginger, milk and sugar. One sip and Richard finds the taste disgusting. He makes no attempt to disguise his feelings.

R: 'What is this? I don't believe that you Indians can drink this tea. Oh my God! There is even a layer of cream floating on top. No way can I have this!'

Words can build bridges or brick walls. How we want to use them is our choice and decision. Bearing the consequences and the results of the choices we make is equally our responsibility.

Thankfully, words are not the only pillar of communication and do not hold up the entire edifice of making oneself understood on a 'stand-alone' basis. Words are supported by the way they are spoken, the style, the manner and the approach. These are the non-verbal aspects of voice and body language.

For any message to be effective, the verbal (words and phrases) need to be congruent with the non-verbal parts. If they are not in resonance and harmony, those listening to us are more likely to trust our non-verbal signals and cues and ignore or forget the words and the substance.

Specifically, *style* comprises the following aspects of the total process:

1. Non-verbal signals and body language. Eye contact, body posture, facial expressions, gestures, muscle flex and tension.
2. The vocal quality. The pace of speaking, volume, tone/pitch, pronunciation, the pauses and even silence.

While *substance* makes up:

1. Words/phrases.
2. 'I' statements used. These express ownership and accountability for one's feelings and thoughts.
3. Reliance on facts as against opinions and subjective perceptions.

Richard's words (the substance) were critical, judgmental and even disrespectful. Such words would definitely not have been spoken with a warm facial expression (body language) or an assertive tone (vocal). Thereby, Richard created a fertile ground for a breakdown of his relationship with his business partner from India.

Words and Phrases Have Intrinsic Power

Often, while speaking, people are confident that they have used the right word to convey what they mean. But they are then surprised when the receiver of their message reacts in a way that was least expected.

The meaning that *we* attribute to a specific word may not exactly be what others ascribe to it! Being sure about the choice of words one uses, and their intended meaning, is essential if one wants to be understood correctly and wants the actual message to reach out.

A few confusing words, to be aware of, are *affect/effect, compliment/complement, insure/ensure, principal/principle, precede/ proceed.* Checking the dictionary for the meanings of words or the spellings and the precise usage of homonyms is a good bet, especially if one is not completely sure. This situation arises when English is our second language and we are not familiar with the subtle differences.

When we are in the selling or persuading business, we need to use powerful and impactful words: ones that 'ring an immediate bell' in the minds of those listening to us! The association with these powerful words is positive and in the English language a few of these are *you, results, money, health, guarantee, discover, proven, safety, save, profits, new, easy* and *have.*

The same is true for phrases. There are a number of powerful phrases that have the power to galvanize, inspire and motivate the listener. Similarly, there are some others that do not appeal to the listener. Such phrases need to be avoided. A few examples are:

- 'Our service is second to none…' (This is not precise but just a statement of 'good' service.)

- 'Now let me give you the facts…' (Means: listen to me or else.)
- 'I hope this doesn't get over your head…' (Conveying to the other that he or she is not intelligent enough to understand it.)
- 'I'm not complaining, but…' (This precedes actual complaining.)
- 'I couldn't believe that you did such a stupid thing…' (Induces guilt and makes the listener feel little and ignorant.)
- 'Let me put it in simple terms, for you…' (Conveys that the listener's comprehension is limited, hence the need to simplify.)

Trust you get the drift!

Non-verbal Communication and Body Language

As shared earlier, the process of communication requires us to focus on the language, words and phrases used to convey our message. And then get familiar with the repertoire of signals that our body sends out, the non-verbal elements of communication. These include eye contact, facial expressions, body posture, the body orientation and movements, hand and head gestures and the body space or proximity between the speaker and the listener(s). Non-verbal communication is referred to as 'body language'.

The most important part to be borne in mind is that our verbal message and the non-verbal messages are *congruent* at all times and consistently complement and reinforce each other.

A doctor advising a patient to quit smoking while holding a cigarette in his hand is in no way going to motivate the smoker to give up his habit.

However, this process is natural and easy if there is a genuine 'intention of communicating and interacting'. It just reflects that. There is no scope for effort, artificiality or acting. If one means what is being said, there is an automatic overlap between the words and the body language. If there is some conflict in our minds, that too will show up. You can be sure that people will read your body language with promptness and completely ignore the words spoken. While we communicate, we are being watched as much as we are being heard.

Our evolutionary experience as a species has given us all the skills and brain power to interpret non-verbal cues very effectively.

Being able to pick up the non-verbal signals of others is a skill that comes in handy to gauge situations and to get indication on how others are accepting or not accepting what we are communicating.

Eye Contact Enhances Trust

Our eyes convey a lot more than we think they do. Looking at a person's face, we immediately turn our attention to their eyes. A glance at anyone's eyes and we can make out if the person is happy or sad. Not only that, if someone says something serious to us, without maintaining eye contact, we are likely to consider whatever is being said with suspicion. Communicating with positive eye contact helps to build trust and rapport.

In a sad person, the pupils are contracted and the drooping lids convey an unspoken sadness, low mood or lethargy. The opposite is true when we are interacting with a happy individual. The excitement shows in the dilated pupils. Combined with a joyful facial expression, fast pace of speaking and brisk movements of the hands, one can be very sure that the person is elated and joyful.

Maintaining eye connect with those whom we are speaking to helps in getting their attention and builds their interest further. It makes them feel important too. It becomes apparent to the receiver of the message that, by ensuring eye contact, you are really making an effort to reach out to them! Obviously, eye contact is not staring into the other's face, but rather a sensitive bonding through our eyes.

In this day and age—when smartphones and hand-held devices yank away our attention every few seconds—the importance of eye contact, while communicating, cannot be over-emphasized.

Healthy, direct and non-fidgety eye contact demonstrates the confidence of the speaker with himself/herself and what he or she is sharing with the other. In addition to that, he or she is transmitting respect and concern for the listener. When one is either unsure or intimidated, the head droops down automatically and the gaze is downward. Even when there is a hidden agenda, and some information is being hidden or deliberately denied, the eyes come forth as 'fidgety' and not relaxed. Rapid eye movements can also be noticed by others.

Our senses are so tuned—thanks to the way our brains have evolved—that they serve like a radar that is receptive to all the vibrations and movements in the eyes. Nothing can escape attention!

Facial Expressions Are a Mirror to the Mind

St. Jerome (circa, 400 CE; an irascible, Croatian Catholic saint) is believed to have said: 'The face is the mirror of the mind, and the eyes, without speaking, confess the secrets of the mind.' This is so true.

Sheena had moved to a new neighbourhood and was eager to make new friends and get acquainted. She met Geeta on one of her daily walks and they got chatting. Geeta was gracious and said, 'Drop in whenever you feel like. We can sit over tea and have pakoras and get to know each other better.' This sounded great and Sheena grabbed the opportunity, and a few days later, went across to Geeta's home. The door opened and Geeta remarked, 'Oh, I didn't expect you. But I am happy you came. Come in.'

The expression on Geeta's face did not in any way, create a welcome feeling for Sheena.

How often do we try to create a facade of an expression that is contrary to the emotions we are experiencing deep within? How often are we successful? The truth is that—unless we are trained for long years in the skills of acting—we can never really disguise our true feelings.

We have more than 70 facial muscles—most of which are controlled involuntarily—that can portray over 7,000 facial expressions! So it is not easy to cover up our expressions, because they are linked in a complex way to the emotions or the kind of thoughts that give rise to these feelings in the first place.

You may pretend to be warm and welcoming, like Geeta, but it will not convince anyone (Sheena wasn't) if the first sudden signal from your face conveys distress!

We all have experienced that a smile puts everyone at ease. A cheerful countenance helps us loosen up and relax our facial muscles. We even look better. Saying 'cheese' while the photographer clicks us has relevance: It makes us smile and then makes us look friendly and pretty too!

A grim look will always alienate us from others. Speakers addressing an audience have been seen to pay more attention to those who show interest in the talk, maintain eye contact and smile! Our face displays varied expressions of confidence, optimism, agitation, anger, friendliness, aggression, nervousness and much more.

At times, we may have to choose to smile even if we do not feel like it. The returns are huge. Besides destressing us, it immediately builds a connection with others. That helps in building rapport, enlisting others and pursuing goals that are aligned.

Quiet Gestures Communicate Too!

Gestures are movements of head, arms, hands and legs, especially as we speak and communicate. These happen naturally and spontaneously and need not be thought out, practised or planned. Being aware and sensitive to our own gestures helps us to read, understand and decipher those of others.

The way people shake their hands while greeting conveys a lot about them and how they are feeling about the other person they are offering their hand to. A confident, full handshake, creating a grip of sorts, sends a warm and friendly message. A weak, limp handshake is mostly adopted by individuals who are unsure of themselves, or maybe they are not interested in the other person. They would rather have no contact with the other and would prefer to get done with the ritual, asap!

Some negative gestures that one observes frequently are arms crossed on the chest. It might, in some situations, convey that we are defending ourselves and are not willing to expose ourselves completely in an honest manner. Shaking our legs or feet, besides distracting the speaker, also shows lack of interest and some degree of disrespect. Playing with and jiggling personal items such as a pen or a pencil, a watch, ring or a cell phone again portray disinterest.

Sometimes this behaviour can also indicate some underlying anxiety and stress.

In rare cases, some people cover their mouths while speaking. The natural consequence is that not all that the person utters can be heard. That might, in fact, be the unconscious purpose of such a gesture: to keep things ambiguous!

A person would constantly use her hand to cover her mouth while speaking. She used to carry important information from one group to the other in the department. So while she would swear that she had conveyed the messages, many would not remember having heard her! Her messages were getting filtered by her inappropriate gesture.

It is interesting to note that diverse cultures and countries have some gestures that we may not be familiar with. Knowing about the differences in the meaning of hand or head positions and other gestures is essential to reduce misunderstandings. If gestures are used in a different culture unknowingly, they can breed strong resentment and can also cause an altercation or a fight.

Postures and Body Space

Just by looking at people and the way they stand, sit or carry themselves, we get considerable insight into and information about how they are thinking and feeling at that instant.

Body postures can either be open or closed. The former shows receptivity to new people, new ideas and a general openness to feedback and views from others. A closed posture conveys just the opposite. It builds more barriers and roadblocks in our communication with others.

While sitting, we could be leaning backwards or forwards. The tilt forward shows an eagerness to know about something and inspires the speaker to share more with an interested listener! If we throw the body weight backwards, the evidence of alertness disappears and conveys a 'laid-back' attitude and even a possible lack of sincerity. One could even come across as being in disagreement with the message being shared.

The degree of muscle tension and ease also 'speaks' to others. A rigid body creates an ambience of anxiety and apprehension.

If we want to reduce the tension within ourselves, a good place to start is to take a deep breath and consciously watch the tension in the muscles and the body melt away!

Body space is the proximity or the distance we maintain with others while speaking to them. When we notice a group of people talking to each other while standing or sitting together, based on how close they are physically, one can automatically infer if they are close to each other or just distant acquaintances. A group of friends who are intimate will be seen huddled together.

As we move to situations where there is a social interaction or a business relationship, we observe that the body space automatically increases. Below is a list of suggested 'distance zones' for different kinds of communication settings.

Intimate zone—No more than 18 inches (< about 40 cm) apart: a mother and baby, for instance.
Personal distance—From 18 inches to 4 feet (0.4 m to 1.4 m): casual and personal conversations.
Social distance—From 4 to 2 feet (1.4 m to 0.7 m): impersonal, business or social gatherings.
Public distance—More than 12 feet (> 4.0 m): speaking at public gatherings.

The more we get to know each other, the more we are permitted into each other's personal space. Large space/distance being maintained is also an indicator of status. Therefore, senior corporate executives, political leaders, directors of organizations are likely to have large offices, big spaces, bigger office tables which automatically increase the distance between them and those they are interacting with.

Voice and Vocal Attributes

While Savita was rehearsing for a lead role in a three-act play, she had to learn a lot about how our voices affect the enactment of our characters. She had to perfect her vocal quality through constant preparation and practice. Besides enjoying the success of the play, Savita came back with powerful speaking skills. Fortunately, for her, the voice training lessons she had been taking came in handy as well.

Two of the key vocal aspects essential for the play were: (a) throwing one's voice; having the voice come out not just by straining the vocal chords but using muscles in the belly and around the diaphragm. Few deep long breaths increased the lung capacity to retain enough air and give strength to the voice. This made the dialogues audible to the audience, because microphones were not placed everywhere on stage. The strain and exhaustion that comes from shallow breathing was much lesser. (b) Modulating and varying the tone of her voice. Here the emphasis was to alter the pitch of the spoken words. This reduced the monotony and ensured the attention of the audience. Who likes to hear the same tenor and treble!

While one may not be a part of a play or a musical performance, learning about the voice parameters is helpful even in our regular conversations. We may not have paid undue attention to, observed or reflected on the basic elements of speaking, but we know their relevance.

Volume, at which we speak, is an important vocal parameter. We need to be audible but not loud. The objective is to be heard clearly. All of us are intelligent enough to gauge the decibel levels that are needed in a certain setting. When talking to one's team in front of a noisy machine, and when there is no choice to delay the dialogue, one may have to raise one's volume. In a theatre while watching a performance or in a library keeping it low and soft would be appropriate and also be appreciated by those around.

Pace or the rate at which words are spoken is also a necessary facet that needs attention. It is preferable to stay within the range of 100–125 words per minute. A slower pace than this would give those listening enough time to wander in their thoughts: A sure recipe for losing them and their attention. On the flip side, too fast a speed would also be a challenge. We need to accommodate for the time it takes to listen, assimilate, process and reflect on the ideas we share. So keeping a tab on how hastily we express ourselves is important.

While coaching presenters and public speakers, we have noticed many speakers rush through their prepared piece. It happens many times because they feel nervous and want to get over with it. Obviously their pace increases, making it hard for the audience to comprehend. Chances of their (listeners) switching off go up. This further worsens their anxiety and that surely does not help speakers.

Pitch and its feature of fluctuating makes it easy for others to follow what we are saying and also enjoy the communication. It helps in getting and then retaining the attention of others.

Imagine a lady who is sharing how much she enjoyed watching a newly released movie. Would her tone be drab or varying? If she was really excited about the film and was sharing her experience, she would be speaking in an animated manner. Would the interest level of others listening to her be high or low? Similarly, when one is narrating a sad incident or speaking at a sombre event, the tone will have a different kind of fluctuation and quality.

A word of caution: When we are speaking in a language that we are not fully familiar with, or it is different from our native language or mother tongue, we need to pay special heed to the pronunciation of the words that we use. While using a certain word, the meaning of which we know and want to convey, it might sound like some other word that has a meaning totally different than what we intend! Such situations can take the receivers off on a tangent, as they say, and the communication will not be the most effective.

Speaking without prior preparation or planning and/or in a language we may not be fully conversant with, one tends to use 'fillers' to tide over the gaps in the conversation. Fillers are sounds or phrases such as 'ah-ah', 'umm', 'aaam', 'you know', 'I mean', 'actually', 'you see' and so on. It takes time for our brains to convert an idea, which we are thinking of, in our familiar language and script and then translate it into the other 'not so familiar' language. That is where the fillers come in. Once we are made aware about their usage and we consciously think what is creating them, we can work on avoiding them.

You Won't Tell, I Won't Ask

On myriad occasions, we have heard people at work and also within families sharing statements such as:

'She didn't tell me that her son got an award at school. And we are supposed to be the best of friends'.

'It would have been nice if my work buddy had disclosed about his new job'.

'The meeting was rescheduled. How come you didn't know?'

'I never received the invitation card to your son's wedding that you had promised me. So I didn't bother to attend!'

These phrases sound familiar, don't they?

As a communications coach and facilitator, Savita keeps on repeating and reminding her clients that if someone in their circle didn't share what they already knew about, why didn't they just ask?

To this query, the most frequent response is: 'Shouldn't they have told me on their own, without any prompting?'

Or

'They are supposed to know what the norms are; why should I have to tell them that?'

Most people fall into this trap of expecting the other to take the first step. However, there is no scope for expectations, or relying on such thinking that usually start with the words 'should' and 'must', if we genuinely wish to nurture happy and healthy relationships. Besides, let's not forget the basic lessons of *intention* and *accountability*. If we actually want that there should be minimal conflict, then we have to take an initiative even when it feels difficult.

Asking questions could take different forms. These could be open-ended, closed, probing or initiating questions. If the purpose is to know and gain information from others, and you think they have more information than you, open-ended questions are likely to be more beneficial.

For instance, 'Which schools are you looking at for your child's admission into kindergarten?' In comparison, asking the closed question: 'Have you started applying to schools for your child's admission?" can elicit either a 'yes' or a 'no' and that will be the end of the conversation. So asking the right kinds of questions is essential to get information, and it does not help to expect the other to 'read your mind' and provide you with all the answers that you might need!

That being said, even if you ask a perfectly well-framed question of another person, you can never be sure to elicit a reply from the other. That is because some people are intrinsically reserved and may not want to share information with you and build a harmonious relationship. So even if you persist, and put forward all kinds of queries, the other could passively dodge them all and may even manage to hide or deny details.

Let us be prepared for such an outcome as well. The satisfaction that you can derive is that as an 'accountable person' (see Section 'Choice and Accountability' in Chapter 1 for details) you have exhausted all options and done whatever was in your power to elicit a response. It is the other's choice not to share and divulge any information and details. So we will happily move on and not try and force things.

Roadblocks to Effective Communication

There are a number of factors that become roadblocks to effectively getting our ideas across. It might be a good exercise to make a note of the impediments that you encounter while communicating or you observe others experiencing them. We have highlighted a few here.

1. *Lack of clarity of the message*: Being sure about what we precisely want to convey helps in getting it across effectively. Thinking it through, in our minds first, and then conveying it helps tremendously. Otherwise, if we think and speak together, there will be many breaks in which we would be mentally clarifying what we want to say. These gaps can sometimes be enough to distract the listeners and give their minds a reason to wander! At times, the lack of preparation will also make us ramble and this too will be a 'put-off' for the observers.

2. *Over communication*: It is definitely important to share the complete story that you have in mind. Sometimes, however, the storyteller takes too many twists and turns and the narrative ceases to be concise. It has been noticed that most people— who are listening—can maintain complete attention for just four sentences. Going beyond that allows enough scope for the listener to either get bored and 'zoned-out' or feel strained by the incessant flow of details and information. This can turn

out to be an expensive bet if we want a specific goal to be achieved. Too much and unnecessary content lets the real message get lost in the surfeit of words.

3. *Over promising and under delivering*: This is true for communications that revolve around the forging of relationships. It is especially applicable to people in the selling business. It is so easy for someone who is selling a product or a service (or making a commitment in a relationship) to convey that their offerings will deliver outstanding features: all within tight deadlines and at optimal costs. However, when it comes to adhering to the commitments made, there is a 'poor show'. Earlier communication is belied, credibility is lost, bitter feelings arise and rapport can be broken. This is true in all kinds of human interactions within families, volunteering groups, small-time businesses, big business dealings and so on. Inflated and overwrought promises are, therefore, an unacceptable road to take for effective communication. If this approach is chosen repetitively and at frequent intervals, there could be a complete collapse of the relationships involved.

4. *Patronizing*: When someone suggests—either verbally or through non-verbal cues—that they are better informed or know more than the other, their communication can be condescending. They may seem to be talking down to the other, and hence, sound 'patronizing'. Even when parents advise their grown-up children to do something in a manner that may seem that the young adults are being treated as children, it can be resented.

The interactions at the workplace are even more complex, since all the parties come with their diverse mindsets, unique experiences, distinct strengths and expectations. There is obviously no scope for patronizing communication, since everyone adds value to the whole: Nobody is above or below the other.

After relocating for work to a foreign country, Radhika made some good friends. One of these friends, Susan, had travelled extensively. In just a few months of interacting, Radhika realized that Susan was communicating from a position where she thought *she knew better how things were to be done*. Interacting with Radhika, Susan started to become more and more patronizing and disrespectful. Radhika was hurt and the friendship turned sour. Finally, Radhika decided to speak up and confront Susan. She mustered her courage and expressed her need to be dealt with respectfully and without being 'talked down to'. This went a long way in repairing the damage that was done earlier, due to Susan's patronizing style.

5. *Excessive use of transparency and frankness:* Some people firmly believe that it is good to be totally truthful and transparent in their communication with all individuals and groups that they interact with. We can empathize with this, since these traits do enable us to feel connected to others and it does foster openness and harmony with those we engage with.

But there is a flip side to this. Being forthright and truthful—without being sensitive towards the other—can be a sure recipe for being misunderstood. Transparency, truthfulness and frankness need to go hand-in-hand with being diplomatic, discreet and sensitive to the process and the receiver's needs. The adage *to call a spade a spade* is not to be followed religiously, without being perceptive of the person/group you are communicating with, and/or the situation. In fact, if you are not sure whether to say something or remain silent, it might be better bet to do the latter.

6. *Reacting versus responding:* This has been covered in Section (A) of Chapter 1 and it might be important to revisit that section again.

It is very important to understand the difference between responding and reacting. When we are uncomfortable with what the other person is saying or the way in which it is said and we feel threatened, we immediately *react*. Our amygdala hijacks our ability to respond rationally! The reaction is a visceral outburst to a perceived 'verbal threat' to our 'well-being'. It happens so that we can defend our views, our actions or ourselves! A reaction is like chemicals interacting with heat and effervescence! There is usually an outburst of emotions. The body tenses up, the heart starts racing and the mind gets ready with a rebuttal to 'get even'.

When one has become aware of the process and the dynamics of the 'amygdala hijack' and decides not to get 'hooked' the next time something provocative is said, even then it seems an impossible task not to *react*! It takes just a few milliseconds for the person to come back to a space of reaction while completely forgetting the endeavour to respond.

In some relationships, people learn what our 'hot buttons' are and they know what to say to provoke us and get us to react! They consciously use this past knowledge to their advantage and expose our worst behaviour, in situations and in front of people where we cannot afford to exhibit this side of ours.

Responding is the skill to listen completely to what the other is saying and to provide an antiphon or a reply only when the idea has been internalized. It comes from a place of more understanding, logic, reasoning and thoughtfulness. The emotional state is also more sober than when there is a reaction. 'Responding' occurs when one uses an intentional *pause* to disallow the amygdala hijack pathway to kick-in, thereby giving the frontal cortex the time to be 'mindful'. The outcome is bound to be a well-thought-out response.

The 'pause principle' helps us to remain centred, calm and aware of our own emotions and those of others. It is a habit that becomes more robust with practice.

7. *Generalizing, exaggerating and stereotyping:* There are many mental biases that we humans suffer from (see Section (A) of Chapter 1). If someone were to focus the 'spotlight' on these mental biases, we would immediately defend our thinking and give reasons to prove that we are right. All of us do this.

Generalizing is communicating using terms such as mostly, many, usually, typically, inevitably and so on; sentences such as '*Many* people from the south are intolerant of us, people from the north', 'Men *mostly* outsmart women in analytical skills' and so on are examples. Stereotyping occurs when we use words such as all, always, never, none, either/or and so on. An example, 'You *never* hear me out, I *always* have to remind you to pick up your wet towel.'

We may have had an experience (a positive or a negative one) in dealing with a specific individual within or outside of our family, from our or another organization, from a host or a foreign country or culture. We tend to remember all such incidents and these cloud our perception, which in turn influence our communication. Our minds are wired, for the sake of survival, to record these associations and experiences and swiftly either generalize or stereotype the person or the event for the next time we encounter a similar setting. This response creates more obstacles and barriers in communicating and relating with others.

Questioning our paradigms, perceptions, thinking biases and distortions go a long way in giving us a fresh and novel perspective to our unique experiences. Not succumbing to the habits of exaggerating, generalizing or stereotyping can work wonders with our communication with people across the board.

(B) Emotional Intelligence

The Four Pillars of Emotional Intelligence

The term 'Emotional Intelligence' (EI) was popularized by Daniel Goleman—at one time a science reporter with the New York Times—when he wrote his bestselling book with the same name in 1995. The book was based on the work of psychologists, notably Stanley Greenspan, Peter Salovey and John Mayer, all of whom had done extensive work in 1989 and later on the concept that humans have multiple intelligences. Daniel Goleman synthesized these ideas and brought them into popular discourse.

EI is defined as the ability of an individual to cognitively perform the following:

1. Recognize diverse emotional states in oneself as well as in others; that is, demonstrate self and social awareness
2. Differentiate between different kinds of emotions and interpret them correctly, and finally
3. Use that information about emotions to guide one's thinking, one's choices and therefore one's behaviour. This implies self and social regulation.

It has now been well established that EI—the ability to gauge, assess and regulate emotions—is a critical attribute of leadership and followership success. Research by Goleman reiterates that

EI contributes more than 2/3rd of the competencies required for effectiveness; as against 1/3rd of the attributes coming from functional and domain expertise.

In the 'ability model' of EI, there are four main pillars. These are:

1. The ability to *recognize emotions*; in one's own body-mind as well as in others. This capacity, when present in an individual, also enables the emotional content of voices, photographs, cultural artefacts and other people to be readily 'picked up' and correctly deciphered. This is a critical aspect of EI, since it enables a person to correctly assess the kind of situation one is in on the basis of emotions.
2. The ability to *rely on emotions to interpret situations* and use this information to solve problems and forge cohesion in groups.
3. The ability to *understand subtle differences in the use of emotional language*; and being sensitive to the differences in emotions as well as to the interconnectedness of certain emotions and finally
4. The ability to *regulate and direct emotions*—especially negative, inappropriate or disruptive ones—in one's own self, as well as in others, and use cognitive skills to manage the emotions, resolve problems and make harmonious progress towards intended goals.

The first pillar of EI requires a person to develop self-awareness, which includes an understanding of one's emotions. Self-awareness and self-mastery have been covered in detail in Chapter 1 of this book.

Practising Emotional Intelligence

Much of what is contained in this book is all interconnected. Can you guess why?

All the skills and competencies that we wish to perfect have to be worked upon by ourselves. Nobody else can make this commitment for self-improvement on our behalf and then work systematically on its elements. The concept of self-mastery, in fact, is all about taking complete responsibility ourselves. Putting EI into practise requires the same degree of personal commitment and drive.

What are the steps for internalizing and then practising EI? We suggest four basic steps that need to be practised at all times to internalize EI and make it a part of your interpersonal repertoire.

Step#1: Becoming *aware* of the fact that we are emotional beings and therefore experience a wide range of emotions and feelings under different circumstances. We need to *become mindful* of these, at all times, as they arise and manifest in our body-mind.

Recognizing that emotions are a reality, helps us to accept them for what they are, rather than become 'enslaved' by them. As long as we live as human beings, facing myriad people and events, feelings and emotions will present themselves. Awareness helps us get acquainted with our sensations and emotions, understand their fundamental source and nature and then deal with them better.

Step #2: Getting *mindful of one's behaviour*. The idea here is that if you are unaware of how you behave, especially when you are all 'fired up', you would be unable to recognize the underlying emotions that stir you to behave in specific ways. Understanding the *'cause and effect'* of behaving helps to demonstrate that one's emotions do play a critical role in one's behaviour and the two are intrinsically connected. More importantly, this step also makes one conscious of the fact that sometimes, emotions can hijack one's ability to rationally think through circumstances. One might end up reacting inappropriately under the influence of a sudden emotional surge and later regret the consequences of that impulsive action. So developing insight and being watchful of one's behaviour is a great source of learning and helps us to regulate our responses, actions and communication.

Step #3: *Assimilating emotions in one's thoughts* is the third step. By watching how the emotions arise in one's mind, one can see that they are much like the waves on the surface of the ocean. They are created by the ocean itself and are a part of the ocean! Our own minds think the thoughts that create the emotions! This is a very fundamental process and in our view assures that no amount of outside provocations or stimuli can alter our emotional state unless we choose (through our own thoughts!) to allow that to happen.

And finally:

Step #4: *Regulating our emotional response and behaviour.* This is the final step in operationalizing EI. We need to use all the awareness that we systematically cultivate about the interconnectedness of our thoughts, emotions and behaviour to regulate our responses to situations. The regulation is essential to be able to live through life—and the myriad social interactions that we have on a daily basis—with peace of mind, joy and a deep inner happiness. Besides, regulation also helps to demonstrate responses that builds lasting friendships, prevents rash or foolish actions and makes us effective in all the diverse engagements and responsibilities that we might be involved with.

When you make it a habit of first internalizing and then practising the four steps to EI, you will notice a remarkable transformation in the manner in which you *connect* with others. Earlier situations that would roil you and bring out unwanted emotions would no longer agitate or irritate you.

It is a new world of ease, peace, effectiveness and accountability that you would be entering.

(C) Active Listening and Empathy

Active Listening: A Magic Key

Anything that is active cannot be passive. As the words signify, active listening is anything but passive: rather it is a dynamic process. A process where the listener is completely involved and is paying attention to both the verbal content and the unspoken, non-verbal cues. There is a high degree of focus and attentiveness.

Where can we begin? As with all things, we start with 'the mind', which is the master of our senses. Focusing the mind and keeping away external distractions and internal thought-wandering helps us to actively listen. The ears and mind are fully open and receptively deployed to ensure that attention is placed on the conversation and the spoken words.

It is not just listening for the sake of listening. It definitely is not a passive exercise. The purpose and the objective are to get the entire message and not lose out on any piece of the communication.

Active listening also encourages empathy in the listener. If individuals are in touch with their own feelings and emotions, they are better able to empathize with the speaker. The common saying 'Put yourself in the other person's shoes' fits well here, but there is a qualifier to it: you can only put yourself in the others' shoes, if you remove your own! So being judgmental, critical, or non-accepting of the emotions shared, have all got to be thrown out during the process of becoming an active and empathic listener.

It is not always necessary for the listener to solve the problem of the speaker or come forward to explain and justify why strong emotions are being felt by the other person. Active listening requires one to just listen! The speaker might have a need to just vent what's bottled up. Flowing with that possible need, without interrupting, responding or resolving the others' concerns, is at the core of an active listening process.

Active listening is truly akin to a magic key that greatly helps in building connections and maintaining them in a way that brings joy and comfort. It is a key that unlocks the maze of rapport-building and simplifies the resolution of differences. Yet, in spite of the critical relevance and need for active listening, at most times this skill is underutilized or completely ignored.

The Eleven Barriers to Listening

There are quite a few barriers that show up as we listen to others. The first step is to be aware about these potential pitfalls and then patiently and systematically work on eliminating them. As with any other skills, honing active listening skills needs practice and perseverance.

Let us now look at some of these obstacles. Take a little time to think through them and determine how you might wish to deal with them, as they come up in you/your responses or when you observe others demonstrate these roadblocks.

1. The listener is either not listening with the degree of attention required or the fitting level of interest. This completely alienates him/her from the situation and those present.
2. The listener is distracted with sounds and noise from varied sources, such as multiple conversations, unending phone calls, operating gadgets and gizmos, television programmes or live performances. It will be so much better to move away from these distractions and invest undivided focus in the real time dialogue and exchange.
3. The listener's mind is wandering. Our mind has an amazing capacity and speed of thinking. It is much like an unbridled horse running amuck! Undoubtedly, it takes conscious energy and intent to get ourselves to the present moment and make the conversation on hand the focal point.
4. The listeners are thinking and planning the possible responses or rebuttals that they would counter the speaker's ideas with. So their mind space is preoccupied with the process of preparing for that.
5. Listeners come with preconceived ideas and assumptions about what they expect will be talked about. Holding on to those notions is comforting to them, but it comes at a cost of not being open and receptive to what comes up. They can be unwilling to explore and/or clarify the narrator's message as it is unsettling to move away from one's rigid stance.
6. The listener's negative emotions and hangovers from some previous interaction sometimes shadow the current, ongoing communication. What happened at some earlier date, and at some other occasion, creates a veil of distortions and the actual message in the 'now' gets diluted or corrupted!
7. The listener's strong personal bias against the speaker, the ambiance or the event. In such a case, the receiver demonstrates selective listening and grasps only that which he/she want to hear. Often they will pick on the most negative pieces of the interaction, missing out all the other positive points.
8. The listener's emotions get ruffled, his/her ego kicks in and enters the situation from the hidden invisible 'back door'. All logic, rationality and an objective, unbiased approach goes for a toss.

9. The speakers may be using language, jargon, abbreviations and terms that are not recognized or understood by those listening to them. The listeners therefore simply 'switch off'!
10. What one is speaking (the substance) and the manner in which it is being said (style) are sometimes not effective. The listeners, once again, 'tune off' or let their minds wander and lose interest.
11. Many a time, groups of listeners begin to have their side conversations. This happens, especially, when the speaker is not able to retain their attention and interest. Their distracting gestures and mannerisms send signals to the narrator that they are happy having their personal story session on the side and that they can do without his 'talk'. This can make the presenter become disenchanted and sort of a vicious cycle gets created that further impairs listening.

Rapport-building Through Attentive Listening

We might have this erroneous belief that if we listen totally and completely to someone, it will communicate that we agree with what is being said. This is not the case. Listening to someone with attention, focus and interest conveys your respect for the other person's right to have a say. It means nothing more and nothing less.

Highlighting distinct benefits of active, attentive listening inspires us to give it a try. It truly is a powerful and an essential skill for rapport-building and resolving differences and difficulties

Some of the key benefits of listening attentively are:

- We get to hear the complete message and appreciate the thoughts and ideas the other is trying to convey.
- The process reduces misunderstandings, confusion and the possibility of misinterpreting words, phrases and messages
- It gently prompts and encourages the one speaking to carry on and complete the entire narrative.
- It stimulates problem-solving. Many more innovative options surface when group members listen actively to ideas and solutions that might be thrown up by individual team members in a creative ideation process.

- New learning takes place. Listening to those who have substantial amount of knowledge and are experts in their domain or sector helps others to gain valuable insights and inputs. Active listening gives rise to a 'transfer' of tacit knowledge that benefits all: the sender and the receiver
- It leads to healthy group dynamics and collaboration.
- For those in sales and marketing, active listening plays a huge role in understanding the needs of the market. It enables feedback from clients, both positive and negative, to be fully assimilated and processed.

It is really worthwhile to devote time to advance and develop this skill. When we first try to work on being aware and mindful while listening to others, we might slip up initially. But diligent effort makes it work. Of course there are no overnight success stories. The more we try, the better we get.

Listening: The Process and the Practice

When we decide to invest time in listening to someone, either at home or at work, we have to be ready and open to whatever comes up. The person we are listening to could have a problem, a certain need, an expectation, a hurting emotion, a new insight or a solution that he/she is keen to share with us.

While dealing with interpersonal issues and resolving differences, some 'bits and pieces' might be revealed that could come as a total surprise to one who is listening. Many a time, we could be the ostensible culprit and hence at the 'centre' of all the emotion and anger felt by the other! So while all that is being put into words—often aggressively, sarcastically or in hurtful tones—one has to be focused and not let go of the 'choice' of listening without responding and of being fully receptive! This can be quite tough initially, but with positive intent and focused practice this ability can be mastered.

For most of us, when confronted with a hurtful or aggressive diatribe from the other, an automatic reaction would be to stop listening and to immediately justify the action or behaviour that the other is cribbing about. But this would immediately end the dialogue. Emotions could get further aggravated, voices could be raised and all efforts to forge any kind of rapprochement would be over, often for good!

We therefore need to be patient and resist the desire to jump in and set the record straight. Through active listening, we have to hear the entire story including the one that is being conveyed only through multiple non-verbal cues. It helps to allow the other to vent their feelings completely and then place the spotlight on the 'real' problem/s. There could be some erroneous assumptions, distorted perceptions, hidden expectations and negative attitudes, on both sides, that active listening can help unravel. Asking questions to probe, clarify and inspire to share more is part of the listening process. If the delicacy of the situation is understood and the individual is respected, a sacred space, where some sort of healing occurs, is created by listening painstakingly.

A set of skills that facilitate moving from generalities in the conversation to specific issues and precise solutions are:

- Clarifying: In any complex or difficult conversation, there is bound to be a need to understand clearly what the actual message is. The person speaking could be confused, have lot of information to share or have unstructured thoughts and content—as they say, be all over the map. In such situations, however proactive the listener, it will be impossible to specifically put together what the speaker wants to communicate. Asking questions, both open ended and closed ended ones (which have detailed or simply 'yes/no', answers respectively) will clarify the points that are being shared. Thereafter, the two-way conversation will be primed to move a notch higher.
- Paraphrasing: This is a vital piece in the listening process and practice. Once we hear a message where a lot of detail and information has been shared, it is always a good idea to take a few minutes to paraphrase what has been heard. This is 'checkback' time. We may have got the communication right (just as it was intended) or we may have missed the point altogether. This is the time to know about it either way and move on.
- Reflecting: This is the practice of enabling our understanding to 'sink in' and be fully assimilated. We take the time to reflect on what we are receiving. At most times we are rushed and

eager to respond. The time spent in thinking and preparing a response needs to be utilized in a deep, meditative and centred approach. This helps immensely in getting a better idea of what has been said and what would be an appropriate way to respond. That we are genuinely thinking through and keenly attempting to get the total picture shows through our non-verbal signals and body language. This is the time to 'pause' and be 'mindful' of what we have understood.

- Encouraging: What encourage speakers are the verbal and non-verbal cues that listeners send their way. An honest desire to connect and respond to the speaker's ideas, builds trust levels with the one who is sharing. Words and phrases such as 'I know', 'I can appreciate', 'We understand', 'What else?', 'How do you know?', 'Are you sure?' and 'What if?', when used by listeners, help in gently prodding and prompting the speaker to express and present freely. Hand in hand with these aspects go the non-verbal components of connecting with the speaker. These include maintaining eye contact, a forward body lean to show we are interested, open (not crossed) arms, gestures to convey openness and flexibility along with a warm, relaxed facial expression. All these mannerisms are spontaneous and are not tutored, of course. They are a direct consequence of our eagerness to know and delve deeper into what is being discussed. When we are in tune, and genuinely want to listen, there will be no need to put on a facade or pretend to hide our intentions. Any artificial approach of trying to feign interest is easily discernible.

- Summarizing: This is putting the entire communication together. The essence of the message is encapsulated at the end of the exchange. The high points are repeated, so that nothing gets missed out or forgotten. Once summarized and confirmed that the speaker's ideas have been clearly comprehended, it is time to put across our perspective and carry on with the rest of the discussion.

Listening, Empathy and Compassion

Actively listening to another individual enables us to *feel the feelings* of the other, as if we are ourselves in the other person's moccasins (that's what Native Americans like to say!). By listening attentively to what is being said, our neurons begin to fire in the brain and start to *mirror the feelings* and the 'inner conditions' of the person whom we are listening to. This mirroring of the other's emotional state is *empathy*.

Empathy, at its simplest, is awareness of the feelings and emotions of other people. It is a key element of EI: the link between self and others, because it is how we as individuals understand what others are experiencing *as if we were feeling those feelings ourselves*.

We can empathise only when we listen with an 'extra' pair of ears. Empathy helps us in relating to others, create bonds and build rapport.

Daniel Goleman identified five key elements of empathy:

- Understanding others
- Developing others
- Having a service orientation
- Leveraging diversity and
- Political awareness

Psychologists have identified three types of empathy:

- Cognitive empathy is to understand someone's thoughts and emotions in a very rational, rather than emotional sense.
- Emotional empathy is also known as emotional contagion and involves 'catching' someone else's feelings so that one can, literally, feel them.
- Compassionate empathy is understanding someone's feelings and taking appropriate action to help.

(D) Communicating Assertively

Assertion

Ranjana, a doting mother, wants to celebrate her son Gaurav's 10th birthday on the terrace garden. She wanted to keep it a surprise for her family and Gaurav too. She spent many hours toiling in the sun to get the space ready for the big day, which was in another couple of weeks. Her parents-in-law knew about her interest and ability to tend to her garden and flowers. So while she was at it in full swing, they thought she was seriously giving the terrace a new look.

A few days before the birthday, she finally shared with her family about the planned party. On the party day, she gets busy with the preparation and when it's time for guests to arrive, they find her father-in-law missing! The entire family waited and waited. Still the father-in-law was not to be found.

Finally, the disappearance was reported at the local police station. Obviously, even as the guests arrived, the party was called off. Everybody was worried and Ranjana was not sure if the party was the reason for the disappearance of Gaurav's granddad. Apparently, the party was the reason. He turned up at midnight. To show his resentment for Ranjana not having taken his permission for the party, he decided to stay away and give his son's family a scare!

How many times have you experienced the inability to put across your point of view to another, because the person whom we are trying to speak to is rude, loud, unreasonable or just unwilling to listen to your perspective? If the answer is 'many times', take heart! You are not alone. All of us have had to deal with people—within our families, among friends, during transactions in the mall or at work—who seem to dominate a conversation and make it difficult to have another perspective brought into the dialogue. Surely it feels bad to deal with such people; and we often experience hurt feelings, frustration, anger and a desire to get even with them 'in future'.

Yet there is hope! We can learn another way of communicating and dealing with such people and situations. And that 'lesser known way' is assertiveness. It comprises a set of communication skills and competencies that come in extremely handy in complex interpersonal scenarios. It helps in dealing with difficult, sometimes unreasonable, people and demanding or challenging situations.

It is not a magical wand to settle all problems but it definitely is a preferred way of interacting and behaving. In the animal kingdom, when there is a conflict, we know of just two reactions. It is either fight or flight. But we humans possess the gift of speaking, which we use if and when there is a disagreement or a difference of opinion. Using this capability can prevent negative conversations and a painful exchange of words.

The basics of effective dialogue, which have been covered in the earlier chapter on communication, apply here too. Here, we will highlight the need to stand up for our legitimate rights, affirm our expectations or concerns, express our opinions or areas of disagreements, refuse requests and say 'no' politely and convey justified negative feelings, anger, annoyance and displeasure.

Putting it simply, assertion is a skill of honestly, openly, directly and respectfully sharing what one wants to. Before the final act of reaching out and delivering the message, it is very essential to know specifically and clearly what one's needs, wants and feelings are. That makes it easy to transcribe them into appropriate words and body language.

A few pointers that help us use the skill of assertion are:

- Using 'I' statements: It is essential to convey our needs and feelings using statements that start with 'I'. For instance, saying, 'I am feeling quite let down and frustrated that I have not been considered for a promotion', instead of 'You did not give me a promotion!' The latter comes across as finger-pointing and blaming, which never helps a cause or attain objectives.
- Immediacy is vital: Encountering the issue and approaching the right person, as soon as the situation arises, is also vital. Delay weakens the case. And with time, many facts and aspects might even get forgotten.
- Specificity: The actual 'problem' has to be exact, specific and clear. That helps tremendously in creating the message in a lucid, crisp and a concise way. This further influences the understanding of the recipient, reduces unnecessary confusion and hopefully decreases the time taken to resolve the concern/conflict.
- Alignment: Making sure that verbal message and words are in tandem and aligned with the non-verbal components. The congruence will happen naturally when we are genuinely involved with the issue on hand.
- Staying unruffled: Last but not the least, remaining calm, cool and centred. It does not take much time for the dialogue to get out of hand and shift from assertion to aggression. And

sometimes for one of the persons to withdraw, get into a submissive mode and leave the situation all beaten up and disappointed. The attitude for assertion has to be 'I'm ok and you're ok' and that goes a long way in keeping the communication respectful, civil and sane.

- Listening attentively: Knowing that listening is not agreeing, helps a lot in being receptive, open and willing to deliberate. Then, assertively solving the problem and coming to a workable comprise or collaborating happens more easily.

Assertion and Other Styles of Communication

While sharing about 'assertion', in the earlier paragraphs, you might have got an erroneous impression that this skill applies only to difficult and demanding interactions or helps in dealing with challenging, unreasonable and aggressive people. That is not the case. Assertion is equally relevant and applicable to positive, healthy dealings and relationships.

One of the key ideas behind the assertive form of communication is this:

Assertive communicators convey to others whatever they wish to in an open, direct and honest manner. They also do so while upholding their own self-esteem and dignity; even as they remain respectful and polite towards the others.

When we feel that something needs to be communicated to others and approach them to initiate a conversation, that initiation is also being assertive. When we give and receive compliments that are genuine, and do so with confidence, even that is being assertive. When we express our affection, appreciation or acceptance, those too are examples of being assertive.

If we are not being assertive, we are trapped in other dysfunctional styles of communication. These could be

- Passive (or submissive) communication
- Aggressive communication and
- Manipulative communication (also known as passive-aggressive communication).

Let's understand these styles of communicating better.

Passive or *submissive* communication occurs when the communicators are operating from a space of feeling inferior or intimidated by the other. They give more emphasis to the rights of others and are therefore willing to 'opt out' even if that is not what they actually want to do. They feel like 'victims' and often think that outside factors (the 'they factors') are responsible for their condition. They are therefore circumspect and afraid to express themselves openly and honestly. They are unable to receive or give compliments easily. Their body language, too, is submissive; they maintain poor eye contact and are likely to speak in soft, often inaudible tones.

People who communicate passively are very likely to hold the following (erroneous) beliefs. Besides, many of their 'self-talk' narratives are likely to be based on these ingrained ideas:

'You shouldn't speak up until spoken to'.
'You must be nice, be respectful at all times'.
'You don't disagree with superiors or express your true feelings to others'.
'Others have rights while I don't have any...' and the like.

Passive communicators, accordingly, exhibit the characteristics of being apologetic while speaking and being generally self-conscious and self-doubting. Besides, they do not express their own wants and feelings and consequently, rarely achieve their goals.

The phrases that one can hear from them are:

'It's alright, Sir, you can please take my share as well'.
'I wish I could do that...'.
'Oh! That was nothing! Anyone could have done that...'.
'Whatever you select for me is fine'.
Passive people typically rely on verbal cues such as 'I wish', 'I can't', 'If only', 'I never', 'I will try', 'I'd better' and 'This may seem silly but...'.

Aggressive communicators, on the contrary, operate from a view that the others have no rights and *can* be treated anyway they like. Their own self-respect and rights have to weigh heavy. As expected, they are loud, intimidating, belligerent, imperious and highly focused on what they perceive as 'winning', irrespective of the adverse impact it may have on the others.

People who communicate *aggressively* are very likely to hold the following (erroneous) beliefs. Besides, many of their 'self-talk' narratives are likely to be based on these ingrained ideas:

'I have rights but you don't'.
'My needs are more important than yours'.
'I am never wrong'.
'People ought to behave the way I think they should...' and so on.

Such communicators are usually loud, demanding, arrogant, domineering, bullying, forceful, arbitrary, authoritarian, punitive, critical, abusive, aggressive in their body language, driven and impatient. They pursue their goals and usually achieve them at the expense of others.

The phrases that they are likely to use are:

'How dare you think like that?!'
'No ifs and buts! This better get done—Now!'
'I veto your idea. It is ridiculous!' And so on.

Passive-aggressive or *manipulative* communicators are the kind who would, if they were not fearful of others, be aggressive people! As they feel powerless in the presence of authority, they are likely to behave and communicate in passive-aggressive ways.

Manipulative communicators tend to be indirect, sarcastic and devious and sulk easily. They tend to blame others for their situation (like passive people) and complain if things do not go their way. They can be unreliable and can carry tales, especially if that 'saves their skin' or helps them 'get even' with the ones they resent.

Their body language, tone of voice and eye contact will be wavering during a conversation and might range from being sweet and friendly to rude and sarcastic. Passive-aggressive communicators think that they are able to disguise their true feelings but this is not often the case. People interacting with manipulative communicators tend to be confused about their true intentions and resent the use of their patronizing or sarcastic language.

Some of the phrases that such people use are:

'I would be happy if you take the lead in this matter—you are the best and my ideas are not as good as yours'.
'You really meant that?'
'How could someone of your calibre think like THAT?!'
'I'm surprised that you don't know what the boss said'.

Manipulative communicators can use any of these or a combination of the following 'styles' while communicating:

* Manipulation by *ignorance*
* Manipulation by *conformity* and
* Manipulation by *guilt*

In all these forms of manipulation, the person whom the communicator wants to 'put down' or get even with is thrown a hurtful comment that is meant to demonstrate that the other is either an ignoramus (Ignorant), a deviant (non-conforming) or someone who falls short on some important count (inducing guilt).

Here are a few phrases that a manipulative communicator might use. Remember, the tone of voice and body language are likely to be sarcastic or even mocking.

'You really mean that you are unable to teach your child the Pythagoras Theorem? And I always thought that you were good at math'. (Ignorance)
'Everybody in the department has agreed to the reorganization proposal! You are the only one standing out like a sore thumb, resisting the generous offer that we have negotiated!' (Conformity)
'Really, Seema, you're the only mother in our group who hasn't yet enrolled her child for swimming classes. Do you want Rohan to become a sissy?' (Guilt)

Apart from assertiveness, all other forms of communication tend to build interpersonal friction and undermine trust—which is so essential for forging rapport. One might even be unwilling to interact with people who are aggressive, submissive or manipulative: because *nobody feels good* after an exchange with such people. They trample on the rights of others and undermine their dignity.

Assertive communication is therefore a skill that is best learned to be interpersonally effective and above all to deal with other kinds of dysfunctional styles.

The Elements of Assertive Communications

As has already been shared, assertiveness or assertive communication is a powerful way of sharing one's feelings, ideas and thoughts with others; but in a way that respects the rights of others as well as one's own. To that extent, assertiveness is aimed at putting forth the facts and feelings exactly as they are, but without necessarily blaming anyone since an assertive communicator realizes that the feelings they feel are their responsibility!

Assertive communicators place the *locus of control* (see the section on Accountability) for their emotions, thoughts and behaviour on themselves. This implies that they appreciate how they feel in certain situations yet they may voice how they feel—directly and politely—in order to let the other party know what they liked or did not like about the substance or the style of the other's communication.

The focus, accordingly, is on being emotionally and socially expressive, so that the communication process remains open, moves towards the intended goal and enables rapport to be built simultaneously. Assertive communicators are sensitive to the feelings of others as well and will ask probing questions to elicit information that will help achieve a common objective. They will also listen with attention and not flit from one idea to another. They will state their limits and know that mistakes may genuinely occur but that is not a calamity.

Their non-verbal language is also appropriate and in line with what they are saying. They maintain eye contact, their body posture is relaxed, the tone of voice is non-threatening and the atmosphere they create while communicating is focused on the intended goal, but is still amicable.

Assertive communicators therefore use 'I phrases' whenever possible, along with sentences that help to move towards a target or solve a problem to the benefit of both parties. Here are a few examples:

'I'm unable to breathe because of the cigarette smoke. I would appreciate if you please smoke outside of the building'.
'I'm unhappy that you did not keep the promise you made to me'.
'I like your sense of dress'.
'I disapprove of the way you are speaking with me'.
'What are the options available to us?'
'I choose to stay here for the benefit of the others'.
'Let's talk things over. I would like that'.

Assertive communicators are generally non-judgmental and they observe the behaviour of the people they interact with, rather than label it. They trust themselves and others and start with the view that all those involved are eager to reach a common goal. They are enthusiastic, confident and have a positive self-concept. They demonstrate openness and flexibility in their interactions. They are typically playful, decisive when needed and have a sense of humour. There is sincerity but not seriousness.

Quite understandably those who interact with assertive people find it much easier to work along with them, solve difficult problems and work as a team. Any endeavour from a person or party to resort to any dysfunctional styles of communication is immediately and effectively nipped in the bud by an assertive individual. They know how to use skills of communicating to defuse any psychological advantage that the other is attempting to derive!

Why Are We not Naturally Assertive?

How often have you seen children—between the ages of 3 and 13 years—driving their flustered parents 'nuts'; asking for something or the other and then promptly demanding something else when the harried parents cave in and meet the initial demands? If the parents take a stand and refuse to give in, there will be loud, noisy, dramatic tantrums!

We have seen a lot of this and are confident that so have you!

Interestingly, such displays of rotten behaviour by otherwise decent kids happen mostly in public places or when there are visitors at home. This is where the kids know how to play things up, since they have gathered early on that their parents will do whatever they want so that there won't be a 'scene' in public, where a lot of people are watching.

There are very few, really aware elders who do not fall in this trap of manipulation and stand their ground. Thereby, they help their children learn about the importance of setting limits and following them as well as managing expectations. Through these and other responses by adults, children also learn that they are accountable for what they feel and how they behave.

As children grow up, they seem to lose their spontaneous voices. From rebellious tantrums, they move into a shell and come forth as submissive. Most of the times, it is the 'significant others', older siblings, teachers, parents/grandparents, other family members, bullies at school and in the neighbourhood, who play a role in hemming children in. They get shut out of conversations and are unable to effectively put across their ideas, feelings and thoughts. Obedient kids are liked by all and if they are pleasing to others, then all the more. But it often comes at a cost: the children have to learn to submit to 'external factors' and that can affect their inner well-being and joy.

Whenever they are in the presence of those, who they think have more power or authority, (either positional or personal) they find their confidence diminishing. They become relatively submissive and find it difficult to assert an idea, suggestion or a proposition.

The ability to communicate clearly and have a grasp of its nuances goes a long way in being assertive. The idea may be crystal clear in our mind, but if we doubt our *communication skills,* we may avoid situations and people, where there is a need to stand up for ourselves. It is really a matter of practice. The more we initiate conversations, the more comfortable we get. So it is always better to face situations and move ahead instead of escaping and hiding.

At times, we expect to *encounter hostility* and because of that *fear*, we drop the desire to be assertive. If we don't even approach the other person, how can we assume what kind of an interaction we will have? Once again, it's better to try than to give up!

Basic Assertive Human Rights

What really goes a long way in helping us to become assertive is getting familiar with the basic *assertive human rights*. Just knowing about them is not enough. Reading through, reflecting on and internalizing them is a continuous process. Referring to them is necessary. Over time these rights would become a part of our automatic cognitive response to situations that we ordinarily find stressful or demanding.

The 11 basic assertive human rights are:

1. The right to take responsibility for the initiation of one's behaviour, thoughts and emotions and handling the consequences that they may perpetuate.
2. The right to state one's limits, expectations and feelings about other people's behaviour in a manner that does not undermine their self-esteem.
3. The right to decide whether one is responsible for solving other people's problems and facilitating the solving of their own problems.
4. The right to change one's mind.
5. The right to make mistakes, to be responsible for them and to learn from them.
6. The right to say 'I don't know'.
7. The right to be treated with respect.
8. The right to explain one's position in a manner that is considered most appropriate.
9. The right to say 'No' without feeling guilty.

10. The right to ask for clarifications about anything one may not understand.
11. The right to ask for what one may want from others, knowing that the other has the right to refuse.

Parroting these statements will not really help. We need to deeply mull on them and mindfully appreciate their importance. Believing in them till they become part of our DNA. As free humans, we are completely entitled to these rights. Communicating with an understanding and appreciation of these provides a sturdy and unwavering ladder for climbing to the assertiveness goal post.

Assertiveness Techniques

To master the ability to be assertive, we need to know about some specific skills and techniques that have to be applied while communicating. The more these skills and techniques are practised, the more effective we get at being assertive.

The common and essential skills of assertiveness are:

1. Saying 'no'
2. Broken record
3. Fogging
4. Negative inquiry

Saying 'No'

One of the more basic skills of assertive communications is being able to take a stand. Many people know how to take a stand—within the family, at work or while with friends—but then change their minds because they feel guilty or otherwise uncomfortable with the feelings that arise when they have to say 'no'.

Knowing that it is our basic assertive human right to say 'no', if we have sufficient grounds not to agree to someone's request, we ought to be comfortable to deny it. Remember, that if giving in to the request would make you uncomfortable or worry about the thing that you have lent (say your expensive Ferrari!), these are sufficient grounds to decline a request.

While practicing assertive skills, we have to ensure what is said (the substance) and the manner in which it is said (the style) are appropriate and do not undermine the self-esteem of the other.

Broken Record

In the 1960s and the 1970s, music used to be sold on black or coloured disks made of a special, hard plastic. These were then known as LPs or 45 RPM records. They would play on a device called a gramophone (in the early twentieth century, soon after Thomas Edison invented it) and later on a record player. A diamond stylus would rest on the spinning record and pick up the musical sounds from grooves that were pressed into the record.

If such a record ever had a faulty groove, the stylus would keep falling back to the old groove and repeat the sound of that groove relentlessly, until the spinning record was stopped or the stylus removed!

This skill is inspired by that condition. In commercial situations, where we need to have our way and where we might find ourselves in a one-time transaction, we can repeat what we want (our goal or expectation) over and over again, even as the conversation with the salesman or the hawker is taking place. The key idea is that we do not get sidetracked by the conversation, but come back to the phrase that we choose to use to convey what we want. If we clearly know what we want, with a little practice it is not difficult to repeat that over and over again.

The most essential part to be kept in mind is to retain a polite and respectful tone of voice. The natural tendency is to raise one's voice, when the other person does not respond the way we expect. If the salesman is a 'smooth operator', he might know how to press our hot buttons and might force us away from the stand we have taken. Holding on to our goal and tailoring our message accordingly, and then politely repeating it, is the essence here. Here is an example of a conversation between a salesman (S) and an assertive customer (AC).

AC: *I bought this thermos flask from you last evening. When I reached home and inspected it, I found the inner vacuum bottle had a hole. I need a replacement for this flask, please.* (Establishing expectation and phrasing what the customer wants: *I need a replacement for this flask, please.*)

S: *Sorry, sir, but we do not replace thermos flasks once they are taken from our store. How do I know that you have not mishandled the flask and are putting the blame on me?*

AC: *I understand that you feel the way you do. I have not mishandled the flask. I need a replacement for this flask, please.* (Not getting side-tracked with the salesman's hint that the client is possibly responsible for the damage. Repeating, like a broken record, the chosen phrase.)

S: *(Angrily) Sir! You are testing my patience! I cannot give you a new flask.*

AC: *(Politely). I hear you. However, I still need a replacement for this flask, please.*

Fogging

Fogging is an assertive skill that helps us to deal with and cope with criticisms and judgments that others make about some aspects of us such as our behaviour, our idiosyncrasies or anything unique that defines us as individuals. The main 'take-away' here is that people make remarks or pass judgment about others, based on their very personal and subjective yardstick of what they think is 'right' or 'appropriate'. Because the world is so diverse and subjective opinions are not factual or based on absolutes, the 'right' perspective of others may be very different from our 'right'! The reference points, as we call them, are different for different people and might not always match with ours. And that is perfectly fine.

So when we get judged and evaluated on the subjective and totally arbitrary yardstick of others, we may not pass muster by those standards. But it is for us to decide, whether we want to follow their benchmark of 'right' and 'wrong' or set our own, because we are unique and have our own minds to guide us!

The skill of fogging helps us to appreciate that all people have their own arbitrary yardsticks; and therefore when evaluated on *that* basis, it is best to simply *agree with the possibility* that there might be some truth in what they say. Fogging does not require us to justify or explain why we are the way we are (no need to explain one's uniqueness). Fogging also helps us to deflect manipulative communication that is primarily aimed at 'baiting us' and making us feel 'downed' or low. Here are a few examples of how fogging is used in conversations.

Critic: 'Hey, why have you stopped dyeing your hair? Grey makes you look so old.'

Assertive Respondent: 'I agree, I do look older than I am.'

Or, another example:

Critic: 'What a rotten sense of dress you have, Bharat!'

Bharat: 'Yes, you're not the first one to notice that!'

In both these examples, the respondent is agreeing with the truth (or the possibility of there being some truth) in the statement. That's it. No further dialogue or discussion is needed. After the response, the critic has nothing further to add!

Fogging as a skill seems easy to use, but initially many find it difficult to apply. The main reason being that most of us are so used to defending or justifying what we do or do not do, that we find it ever so difficult to simply accept the fact that there might be some truth in what the other is perceiving. With practice however, fogging can be a liberating skill and can bring great freedom from the tyranny of manipulators and those who are critical of us and want to put us down!

Negative Inquiry

As humans we all make mistakes. We learn from them. Yet, many of us are so overwhelmed by the fact that an error has been made, that we are unable to perform effectively or assertively accept that while we are sorry for the mistake, we are keen to learn from it and move on.

The fifth item on the basic assertive human rights list states that *we have the right to make mistakes, be responsible for them and to learn from them.* This right is at the heart of the skill of negative inquiry.

When we have actually made an error, it is important that we acknowledge that fact. If need be, we report to our team or our superior and accept the occurrence as another opportunity to learn from.

That said, often an error may be pointed out to you by your superior or your team leader. In that case, they may also use the opportunity to settle scores with you and are likely not to take the error lightly. They might wish to humiliate or 'down you' by raising their voices and be abusive.

As a problem-solver, you are keen to learn about what you did not do right and, accordingly, seek feedback about that. Especially, if it helps to find out more about the mistake.

But often, even before we have had a chance to determine the right way forward, we get into a defensive mode and justify our actions. That further gets in the way of dealing with abusive, unhelpful feedback.

The basis of negative enquiry is the attitude of accepting that one can 'goof-up' and it is alright. Of course, in a job one cannot just keep on making the same mistakes, but things may not always go as planned despite attention. So in such situations, the skill of negative inquiry helps in reducing the guilt associated with making an error by finding out what can be done to rectify the issue and take remedial steps. Asking questions to clarify and then listening carefully to the superior (or expert, as the case may be) helps the inquiry process. The last part of the process is to be accountable for the decisions taken and take action, as agreed, within the time frame that is mutually set.

Clinging to Conflict

Bharat noticed a peculiar situation at a busy airport one late afternoon.

Two travellers, who had just arrived from somewhere, were waiting for their bags at the carousel along with hundreds of other fliers. A few minutes later, one of the travellers picked up a black stroller off the belt and began walking away; confident in the knowledge that he had got his checked in bag.

However, just as he was about the leave the terminal, another traveller ran to the first one, shouting loudly and angrily 'that's mine, my bag, my bag! Stop!'

The first traveller was startled. He stopped and looked at his bag and then the tag on it. It was then that he realized that he had walked away with someone else's bag! He turned to the other person, maintaining eye contact, and in an assertive but polite tone apologized for the mistake and that too profusely. He kept on repeating the phrase, 'I'm sorry, this was an honest mistake! Really sorry, it was just an honest mistake!'

The angry traveller, however, was in no mood to hear any of that. He held on to the other man's arm and as he walked him back to the belt, he shouted:

'You were stealing my bag! Your bag is by the belt and you didn't take it, but took mine instead!'

By this time, the two were back at the carousel. Curious onlookers by now had guessed what the commotion was about. When they took a look at the two bags, everyone was amused because the two were exactly the same size, colour and model!

So it was a mistake after all. Anyone could have erred.

But that's not how the angry traveller felt. He just went on and on, allowing his angry emotions to take a grip over him. He badgered and heckled the other traveller all the way to the parking lot!

What exactly was happening out here? Obviously, one man made a genuine mistake; and when he realized that an error had occurred, he assertively apologized and thought that the matter was over.

The other man, however, kept on clinging to the conflict. He just wasn't willing to let go and move on from the situation—which had been resolved anyway when both the parties got what was legitimately their stuff.

Assertive people do sometimes encounter others who are unwilling to move on even after a problem has been solved and everyone's 'basic assertive human rights' have not been violated.

Another extreme situation arises when a very submissive person is unwilling to resolve a problem and avoids interacting, letting the problem fester. Both avoidance and an unwillingness to let go can be spoilers in the amicable resolution of problems through assertive interactions.

People who are emotionally intelligent know when to let go, to forgive and to move on. They also know the importance of engaging with others to deal with or confront issues that cause conflict. But those who are contentious, or have a habit of avoidance, tend to either cling to conflict or stay clear of it. Either situation, however, can be handled well through assertiveness.

SIMPLE STARTING STRATEGIES

Interactional Excellence

✓ Know that you are unique and special and there is none other than you in the whole cosmos.

✓ Examine your intentions before you enter into an engagement. What do you really wish for? Is that what you would be communicating as well? Are you being true to yourself?

✓ Learn to listen with attention and empathy.

✓ Become a collaborative, team-playing problem-solver, rather than a confrontationist.

✓ Ensure that your verbal and non-verbal communications are always congruent. This helps to build trust and makes you come forth as being trustworthy.

✓ Enrich your interactions by consciously working on how you communicate with those whom you engage with.

✓ Learn and master the techniques that make for effective communication: be it in a one-on-one situation or where you are making a presentation to a large gathering.

✓ Practice makes perfect. The more you practice, the better you will get at interacting with others.

✓ Learn the basics and the skills of assertiveness. Practice these in as many situations as you encounter until you attain mastery in their use.

✓ Internalize the basic assertive human rights.

(E) Queries and Responses for Chapter 2

How can one initiate a conversation with someone with whom one does not have any apparent common interests?

The process of starting a conversation with a stranger, or a new acquaintance, requires what your question also suggests, namely initiative! It implies you take the lead to introduce yourself and provide the other person some 'free information' about yourself (see Section 'Communicating Assertively'). This might set the conversational ball rolling. Once you have made a beginning, it will help to listen carefully to what the other is sharing. Being totally present and observant of both verbal and non-verbal cues, you might learn about some common interests that you have. Putting across your thoughts and points and listening to his or hers will help the conversation to move forward progressively and an adequate level of interest and stimulation will also be built.

If that does not happen despite your initiative and persistence, then no need to waste your time. Instead engage with other eager conversationalists, making sure that you choose topics that are neutral (as against emotive). Talking about points that provoke others can lead to an emotional showdown, rather than an enjoyable tête-à-tête!

Sometimes, especially in large gatherings, it might seem as if everyone is so engrossed in talking within their little groups that 'barging in' seems impolite. But here, too, you can wait for your chance and then make an entry. We must admit that at times just being with yourself—quietly watching the *schauspiel* around you—can also be quite relaxing.

How can I communicate with my superiors without feeling nervous?

In organizations and cultures where hierarchy is valued and where the senior person is also advanced in years, it can get demanding and difficult to communicate upwards. However, in spite of trepidation and anxiety, one can learn to do it if the following pointers are kept in mind.

1. Superiors prefer focused and short messages, since time is a valuable resource for them. It helps to be brief and to the point.
2. It is desirable to speak unflinchingly and with confidence, with the right vocal quality as well as appropriate body language.
3. If you think you would be unable to speak before your superior effectively, you might prefer to send him or her an email or a memo instead. The receiver might give the written word more attention, rather than trying to understand your thoughts. That too might have the desired impact (See Section 'Communicating Assertively').
4. Just because you have shared your thoughts with your superior does not mean that what you asked for will be granted. However, you will feel good about yourself that you decided to take up the issue with your senior, as it was important for you. That feeling is essential for building long-term well-being and effectiveness.
5. As with all other skills, practice makes them perfect. The first time the impact of your conversation may not be as desired. However, that should not deter you from speaking to higher ranking officials, at another time and another date.

How should one deal with colleagues at work who take undue advantage of you?

Interactions are an essential element of being a part of our world. Even if we wished, we cannot run away from them.

If your colleagues are taking undue advantage of you, we presume they impose unrealistic expectations on you and they believe that you have got to deliver on them.

However, you have a choice. You can state your point of view in a way that is direct, honest, respectful and assertive. You can make it clear that much as you believe in working together, there is a need for an equitable distribution of workload. This has to be done without aggressively putting down your colleagues, for what you think is their 'unfair' stance on the work they expect from you.

The choice of words used to convey this (the substance of your message) as well as the manner in which they are conveyed (the style) are both essential elements of communicating assertively on the matter. When you do this, you are establishing that you understand that the work has to be accomplished, but are unwilling to be weighed down with more than a fair share of it.

In the long run, this assertive, direct and honest approach—wherein you respect your rights and those of the others—will be appreciated.

How can I say 'no' to those who are trying to push me into something that I know I am not ready for?

The ability to say 'no', emphatically, is a critical life skill and needs to be learned without delay. We would suggest that while you read this response of ours, please do visit the Section, 'Communicating Assertively'.

There would be countless situations in the course of one's life, where one has to stand up and say 'no' to those who might be trying to push you into situations that you may wish not to get into. This is not just confined to formal or official situations: Such situations can arise even amongst friends, one's family or between colleagues at work or while socializing.

The key ability in being able to assertively convey that you are unwilling or not ready for something is to express how you feel about the situation, using 'I' phrases. For instance:

'I do not feel comfortable doing this task.'

'I understand that you would like me to do this job, but I am already tied up with working on the marketing plan and would not be able to do it within the time you expect.'

'I know you have a date and wish to borrow my car, but I'm sorry I am using it tonight.'

'I have promised my spouse that I will be back home by 6:00 pm today and would not be in a position to handle this now.'

There might be times when you think you are not ready for a role or an assignment at the workplace. You could take your superior into confidence. Together, you would need to address any deficit in competencies or skills and work through a plan of learning and development to ensure your preparedness in a specified time frame. Taking your superior's help once would be okay, but you cannot do this regularly. People might think of you as one who is a 'shirker' and unwilling to get into the bustle of the workplace.

What would be a polite way to convey that I do not wish to be disturbed when I'm in a bad mood?

If you are in a bad mood, chances are that those around you will pick the non-verbal signals and stay clear of you! Nonetheless, if you really wish for people to know unambiguously that you would not like to be disturbed—while you are not feeling good—you will have to convey this in a direct and open manner.

As we have shared in the Section 'Communicating Assertively', you have a right to state your limits. But we need to reiterate that the style needs to be appropriate, where the self-respect of others is maintained. For example, use of the right words and the right tone of voice. 'I' phrases go a long way to express our desires and to state what you wish the others to do:

'I would appreciate if I am left alone for some time today, please.'

'I would request that I not be disturbed for the next three hours, please.'

As against these, aggressive phrases such as the ones discussed further convey your feelings most inappropriately. In fact, if anyone had any doubts about your being in a foul mood, the content and the tone will be a complete give away! And besides that they are bound to alienate you from others around you.

'Can you leave, now!'

'Can't you make out that I'm upset and don't want to see your face?'

'Why are you being so intrusive?'

Don't forget that it is *you* who is experiencing a foul mood; and blaming others for your misery will further annoy you!

How can one deal with people who pass judgement and make critical personal comments about you, without even knowing you?

One does meet people who have a tendency to make comments and unflattering remarks about others, including those people whom they may not know well at all! Often such people are just having a little fun and are also trying to gauge if you're the kind of person who can play along with some humour or are someone who gets riled easily.

If you can sense from the tone and intention that words are being said in jest, with no malicious intentions, then it will be easy to stay light-hearted. However, if what is being said is critical, judgemental and hurtful, then you will have to stand up for yourself and make it clear firmly and assertively that you do not approve the mode of communication. As always, rely on 'I' statements:

'I do not like the way in which you are speaking to me. I would like you to stop, now!'

'I dislike the mocking tone in your voice, even as you're speaking about my good qualities. I would like that you do not speak to me for now'.

Being assertive might also be necessary with people who are close to you and who have known you for a long time—your siblings, colleagues, buddies and so on. There is nothing wrong in stating, even to such people, what you do not like. Close friends, bum-chums and relatives also have to respect your 'space'. Because those who are close to you and know you well are the ones who can touch your 'hot buttons' more often than not. All the more reason for being assertive!

My father wants me to join the family business whereas I wish to study further and pursue a master's degree abroad. What can I do to have my way, without my relationship with my father getting affected?
Since the objectives here are divergent, there is bound to be some interpersonal abrasion and friction in the interactions between your father and yourself.

Parents usually have the best interests of their child in mind, when they make plans for them. It is also true that children, especially as they go into adulthood, have their own wants and preferences. They are more aware of the current trends and what their peers from this generation are thinking and achieving. Parents, on the other hand, may be relying on information that is dated and no longer relevant.

The best way to resolve the situation, therefore, might be to have a face-to-face conversation, a dialogue that would help to put forth your perspective. For example, stating clearly but politely how pursuing your dream of studying further will contribute to your happiness and well-being. Your father may be harbouring a set of concerns and worries, such as who will fund your studies, what you would do after your complete the coursework, will you be lured to stay back in the foreign land forever and would be hitched to a girl while you are there. You will benefit by first listening fully to his apprehensions and fears and then calmly putting across your perspective on the points raised. Brushing them under the carpet will keep the flame simmering. In the best interest of upholding the relationship, and you pursuing your dreams, respond preferably with facts and data and reassure your dad.

I experience fear every time I have to speak to a group in an unfamiliar setting. What can I do about this?
The fact that you are aware about your experiencing 'fear' is a major step towards learning how to deal with it. Fear is an emotion that has helped all living creatures survive and thrive, by serving to energize the body to either run away from danger (the flight response) or to attack the source of fear (the fight response). In humans, too, fear is an innate response to dangerous or risky situations. However, in non-threatening situations, experiencing fear can be limiting.

Being emotionally intelligent means recognizing the emotions that you experience and then regulating them in a way that you continue to be effective.

It is normal for any presenter, even for seasoned ones, to experience fear for a bit when they are speaking in an unfamiliar setting. Is this reassuring? Even asking for a clarification and drafting a question in a formal meeting can be a source of anxiety. The unease could be coming from the assumption that others will think of you as being ignorant for posing this query or may grill you for 'rocking the boat'. Presence of hierarchy can also make us experience anxiety while we wish to direct a legitimate question at our superiors.

Most of the underlying 'self-talk', that gives rise to fear and anxiety, is based on flawed/erroneous assumptions and logic and need to be disputed.

One can deal with fear of speaking in groups, or larger audiences, through this simple checklist:

- Treat the audience as your ally
- Remember, you are the expert (or the person called upon to speak)
- Prepare, prepare and prepare
- Become familiar with the setting and the equipment that you will be using
- Work on self-defeating self-talk; shine a positive light on your abilities.

Is it essential to work on forging intimate relations that are lasting or can one just breeze in and out of these?
For lasting relationships, it is essential to communicate effectively, share feelings openly, listen actively, be sensitive and respectful of others' rights and needs as well as demonstrate social graces and etiquette. These help to build trust and a robust foundation on which the relationship can stand 'tall'. The same rules apply for forging intimate, loving relationships. With just one rider. What makes intimate relations different is that there is a high degree of physical and sexual contact. The body language, body space/proximity, gestures and movements exude warmth and affection. While sex plays an important part in the enhancement of intimate relations, it is not as if intimacy requires just frequent sex. One could indulge in sexual acts without being intimate also.

Besides the external display of emotion of love through holding hands, hugs, kisses, leaning on the shoulder and so on, for the relationship to last, there has to be trust, loyalty and empathy between the partners. This requires making time to be physically close to each other, caring for each other's needs and expectations and consciously working to make it click, even when the going seems tough.

Having a trusting relationship also means that you would not develop intimate relations with someone else, while you are already in a relationship. However, if you and your partner both articulate and agree that you are living together only for convenience and do not wish to be bound to one, or two sexual partners, then that is a choice that you can exercise. However, in our view that is a slippery slope to be on and one cannot forge a lasting, trusting relationship with your partner if you are also searching for others to sleep with. The consequences—whatever they may be—will be a result of your choice.

I have noticed that some senior officials in organizations lie through their teeth! What can be done about this?
Our world is made of people and the problems that they come with: people problems. Organizations are no exception. Accepting this fact helps in dealing with the frustration that we feel at finding people behaving unethically or dishonestly.

Expecting senior officials in organizations to behave and respond truthfully at all times may be desirable and we all would like that; but it is an unrealistic expectation. This belief can trigger frustration, anger and annoyance.

To deal with such situations there are three aspects that one needs to keep in mind: Remain mindful of the way the senior officials are behaving, so that you do not get ruffled or exasperated by their inappropriate behaviour. Second, use the skills of communicating assertively (see Section 'Communicating Assertively') to tackle such people, so that you get what you want from them; but more importantly, you do not get embroiled in their lies or deceitful ways of working, by being naive or credulous. Finally, if you think some laws have been broken by your superiors, or some wrongdoing is occurring under their watch, which you have evidence for, you would definitely need to 'blow the whistle' and report the matter to the ethics counsellor or other authorities within the organization or law enforcement agencies outside.

If a goof-up at work occurs because of a fault of my supervisor, I get all the blame! How should I deal with this, without affecting my relationship with my supervisor?
This is a tricky situation that can occur at the workplace, although it is not as uncommon as one would expect! The flip side is also common: when the supervisor takes all the credit for whatever is going well in his or her team.

Dealing with this situation is best done in one of the regular team meetings where the lapse is being analysed. You can state your points with the intention of ensuring that similar (or the same) errors do not recur. At no point in time must you endeavour to show your supervisor 'down'. No abusive language is to be used, nor should your tone be loud or threatening. Your body language, too, must be congruent with your intention—which is to point out the real reason for the error to have occurred.

In doing so, you would have clinically drawn attention to the causes of failure and ensured that a light is cast on any of the factors that have to do with 'people'. This would be quite adequate to get the matter off your chest, without deliberately trying to wreck your relationship with your superior.

Another option is to meet your supervisor one-on-one and, again, let him or her know politely and directly that you are upset that blame for the error is being foisted on you. You could state that you value your relationship with him or her, but his or her habit of placing the blame on you for something that you are not responsible for, is unacceptable to you.

It can happen that the supervisor may—despite your being respectful and assertive—find your actions of airing your feelings in the meeting, and even with him or her in person, inappropriate. He or she may even upbraid you for being 'arrogant', 'a tattle tale' or someone who is a sissy and not tough 'like the others'! All these are perceptions and thoughts emanating from your supervisor's mind and have nothing to do with you. You'll have to learn to fog such comments! (See the Section 'Communicating Assertively'.)

How does one point out mistakes in a person's work, without insulting his or her intelligence?
Giving and receiving feedback is an essential part of working together. One has to be careful, however, in the way constructive suggestions are communicated. If the manner is too critical, even well-meaning feedback can morph into criticism and one can be sure that the other person will be least receptive!

Feedback has to be objective. Merely saying 'You made a mistake' is not helpful to the other side, because it does not convey *why* a mistake occurred. Instead, if you were to say something on these lines it would be helpful:

'The report that you presented to the Vice President today did not adequately cover the demographic details of our target market.

I would have liked you to offer more data on the spending patterns of the different age groups within our market, so that we could have planned our product positioning on that basis.'

Here there is more data on why the report fell short and what might have been done to make it more useful.

For feedback to be effective, therefore, any comments and observations have to be based on the recipient's professional work. They also must be specific and helpful in stimulating improvement. If the person being given the feedback thinks that the other person is simply using the platform of giving feedback to attack and denigrate, the session will be a disaster.

The primary purpose of giving constructive feedback is just that: giving data and insights to others, so that beneficial change can be made by them.

The manner in which the communication goes, in terms of the verbal and non-verbal signals that the giver of feedback reveals will influence the receptivity and the responses of the other.

Any fruitful feedback conversation ideally leads to necessary and desirable changes. When conveyed in a way that is relaxed, positive and focused, the efficacy is considerable. Just remember that giving meaningful feedback is not a thing to be done casually, and not only when an error is discovered. It might be desirable to have another set of face-to-face feedback meetings to sensitize the other on the areas of improvement, and then stimulate that the person works through the problem or the specific concern with a corrective action plan.

3

The World of Work

(A) Serving, Managing and Leading

Good Work, Dull Work

Let us play an imagining game. Think of yourself as part of a group of hunter-gatherers about twenty thousand years ago.

What would your day look like? If you were a young man of 16 years of age, you would probably join the older members of your family group to hunt for food. Before the hunting expedition, the men would collectively frame strategies on where and how to hunt. All the members would prepare and sharpen their weapons and then await the signal for the hunt to begin.

If you were a young woman, you would stay back in the cave dwellings and join the other women of the extended family to ensure that the animals brought in from an earlier hunt were skinned, the meat separated from the bones and the pelt given to another group of women to make into body coverings. Some other women would be suckling and taking care of the babies and young children. The rest would be looking after those in the community who were either sick or hurt. A few younger girls would be shaping soft bones and teeth into combs and necklaces.

So, much of the work of early humans was aimed at surviving and protecting their families and children from the elements, predators and enemies. Even while focusing on these primary aspects of their work, time was taken out for bonding with others, as well as children. Stories were told, heroic exploits recounted and collective meals were cooked to feed everyone.

The joy in early human gatherings came from fellowship, from having sufficient food that was adequate for all to survive and feel nurtured as well as from leisure time spent with women and children, sharing tales and learning the skills of carving bone, making whistles of reed and drums of animal skin stretched on hollowed-out trunks of trees. The task of hunting was critical since it enabled the early humans to collect enough food to survive. But even then, whenever there was surplus of food and adequate protection from the elements the real joy came from family and fellowship as well as from bonding and sharing stories and music.

If work was not done by the members of the commune, they would not survive. The work of all in the commune was, therefore, focused on something as *meaningful* as survival. Individually and collectively the efforts of all contributed to something that was truly very important. The work would also have yielded a great deal of fellowship and engagement with others. All members would have had sufficient autonomy to pursue their own interests (making weapons, discovering new caves, tracking beasts and playing games) and derive joy and satisfaction from being alive.

By the time we get to the twentieth century, we notice a completely fragmented approach to work. Thanks to the ideas of capitalism, human motivation and maximizing the fruits of industrialization, the prevailing view that gained ground was that humans had to be pushed to work, and it did not matter how they felt as long as they made the things that would maximize the benefits of the firm. Industrial society, therefore, designed human systems for high levels of throughput, breaking jobs into small parts and incentivizing 'lazy' people to produce more and more of those small parts using money paid for every good piece made. A Charlie Chaplin movie called *Modern Times* (1936) captures the prevailing sentiments poignantly.

In the light of this, it should come as no surprise that despite all the progress that we may have made on various fronts, modern human societies have somehow lost the link between work and the factors that contribute to making that work meaningful. People are unable to see themselves contributing to goals that are larger than themselves and which serve the greater good.

This is one of the reasons why people these days find work to be so uninspiring. In fact, one does not have to look far to see how apparently sensible and educated young men and women are willing to give up well-paying but 'routine' and sometimes 'boring' jobs to take the plunge, fighting as mercenaries or terrorists for a 'cause'. Where a purpose and the connected goal—irrespective of how brutal or ugly it might seem to others—has the seductive power of *seeing* larger than life, it can suddenly inject a heavy dose of *meaning* and *purpose* in an otherwise vapid and insipid life. It is this sentiment that many violent groups rely upon, to recruit young and immature men and women into violence and wars in distant lands.

So the reality is that we work because that is how we have evolved. Working is essential for us to be human. Furthermore, if we are not committing ourselves and deploying our uniquely wonderful skills and talents to deliver outcomes that are valuable to society and our planet, then we are unlikely to be satisfied with our work.

However, if we know that we are doing something big, helpful and useful to society, and are using our talents in the process, it can be extremely enriching. Within the deeper levels of our interiority, we would perceive our work in a way that gives a lasting feeling of joy, fulfilment and satisfaction.

It has been rightly said that even if one is the president or prime minister of a country, one may yet feel that one has the lousiest job on the planet. On the contrary, a simple farmer working in his fields, a butcher or a miller (like the one in the famous poem 'The Miller of the Dee' written by Isaac Bickerstaffe in 1762, as part of his play 'Love in a Village') might all be more joyful and relaxed about the work they do and the lives they lead.

If the money that we get from our work (the hunt or the cultivation) is not quite as high as we would want it to be but we and others *believe* that the work we do has meaning and a definite socially beneficial purpose, even then the activity can be a source of joy and happiness.

So what does all this have to do with us?

We need to view the work we do, not in terms of its outer aspects (the salary, the hours, the kind of interactions with the boss and so on) but rather in terms of how much of our inner-dimension is aligned with what we are doing and how it relates to life.

So to recap: We work because work provides our lives with *purpose* and *meaning*. It gives us a chance to use our interests and skills to *serve* others and make for a better world. It provides us a means to *engage* with others, form bonds of *friendship* and *collaboration*, and derive monetary and other rewards that help us to feed and clothe ourselves and those who depend on us.

That said it needs to be emphasized that we can *create* our own work that fulfils most of our aspirations.

Work in Flux

The world of work is changing at an unprecedented rate.

More than half the kinds of jobs that were done by people merely 30 years ago are no longer done any more. Jobs and roles that exist today would vanish after another five years or so. Digitization and robotics will transform the factory floor, enabling fewer people to produce far more output and with considerably more accuracy than ever before. Full-time jobs will, therefore, be fewer and job security too is likely to diminish.

What does this mean for young professionals?

It implies that we have to consciously create work for ourselves based on how we can best use our skills and talents to serve the needs of people. We will also have to continuously *renew* ourselves and ensure that we are equipped to serving a legitimate societal need. This is the bottom-line. Nobody can predict the way the world will evolve precisely, but some trends are already apparent. It helps to be riding ahead of these trends and being in a state of preparedness for any of the future transitions that will occur.

When work is underpinned on the idea of serving others and leverages the skills and competencies that you would like to use to serve others, there is bound to be a wholesome outcome.

All Work Can Be Enjoyable

One of the powerful lessons of living a life of joy, purpose and ful-filment is that the feelings of well-being, happiness and satisfaction have more to do with our own *interiority* rather than the conditions outside of us. That is, much rests on our approach to the experi-ences we have: our attitudes related to things, our values and the kind of self-talk we allow to play out in our heads. This applies also to the kind of work that we might do and on how fulfilling it feels.

In simple terms what this means is that if we have chosen a vocation that we really like, or are passionate about, the chances are that even when the work becomes routine we would be able to derive a sense of fulfilment from it, provided our inner-dimension is in a state of balance and harmony. Yes, there can be jobs that are difficult, poorly paying or the kind that you may not intrinsi-cally enjoy, or one may be in an organization where the culture is exploitative and the superiors are mean-minded and unfriendly. Such conditions are bound to affect the way you feel about the work you do. But if you have *chosen* not to quit and work some-where else, then as long as you are in that vocation you might as well tune your interiority so that however tough the circumstances are, you still feel at ease and as happy as you choose to be.

It is this idea that is captured in the phrase 'work is worship'. The notion that this phrase reinforces is that if *any* work is done in the *right* manner, and with the right attitude, it can have the uplift-ing qualities of prayer. Sometimes incredulous young professionals find this rather bizarre. 'How can that be?' they wonder.

The fact is that this idea is anything but bizarre. Choose the right thoughts and approach your work with a 'different pair of eyes', and then watch the magic unfurl!

The Misery of Sisyphus

Every organized human effort requires that once a goal has been reached, one would like to maintain that level and that standard. This is as true for rudimentary tasks and organizations as it is for complex ones.

The absence of an ability to hold on to a desirable position or goal that is achieved after some effort is reminiscent of the mythical Greek character Sisyphus. According to legend, Sisyphus was the son of King Aeolus, who at that time ruled over the ancient kingdom of Thessaly. Sisyphus himself was a cunning, wicked man who used his craft and deceit to become the founder and the first king of the Kingdom of Ephyra. He ruled with cruelty and an iron fist, and so infuriated the Gods of Ancient Greece (Zeus, especially) that they punished him by forcing him to roll an immense boulder up a high hill only to have it roll down to the base once again. Sisyphus had to continue this task for eternity because his boulder would never maintain its new position at the top of the hill.

Many organizations find that improvements—which are achieved in areas of critical performance or in key metrics and usually through the work and efforts of 'champions' or teams of motivated people—slip back to the original state the moment the enthusiastic employee(s) move(s) on to another role or a different function or department. This occurs because the gains are often not held by making permanent the processes and systems required to function at the higher and improved level.

Holding the gains is, therefore, an essential requirement of our organized endeavours if we do not wish to emulate the misery of Sisyphus. This requirement also implies that there is a need to direct the proper use of human effort as well as the deployment of the right resources, processes and procedures to ensure that whatever we set out to maintain is permanently 'held' at a new, desired level.

Dr Joseph M. Juran (1904–2008), an American engineer and later a consultant, was one of the world's leading authorities on quality. He wrote a seminal book on this topic in the early 1960s, entitled *Managerial Breakthrough* (1964).

In this work of his, Dr Juran suggests that managers in organizations typically work hard to keep things in a 'state of control'— which is definitely desirable but will not, on its own, yield to significant improvements. Juran also popularized the concepts that came to be known as the 'Juran Trilogy' wherein he clubbed key organizational actions as 'quality planning', 'quality control' and 'quality improvement'. Dr Juran was of the view that all three aspects were essential for the success of organizations but required a differential set of managerial processes and structures to achieve notable attainment in each.

Managing: Keeping Things Steady

Managing the elements of keeping things in a state of control and maintaining standards and performance metrics at the desired levels are essential for any enterprise. In this day and age, when we wish to mass-produce goods as well as services that are identical and which are also produced at optimum and predictable levels of cost, organizations do want to keep matters steady and parameters that are not 'out of control'.

Successful organizations around the world spend considerable sums of money on talented people, equipment, sophisticated hardware and software to create responsive systems that can swiftly predict how key parameters are behaving. During performance reviews, management boards and committees of senior executives in organizations look at how the performance of parameters compares with targets, standards and key values. When things are steady and as predicted, everything is 'in control' and people are normally happy with this.

This is 'managing' at its best. All parameters are steady, there are no disruptions and everyone is in a good mood. If there is an adverse change in a key parameter, all managerial resources will quickly be directed to the problem so as to fight any emerging fires. When things return to normal, resources are withdrawn and all is likely to be forgotten until the next crisis.

Typically, if one does not get to the root of a problem and determine why some parameters are drifting, the problem is bound to occur again. Managers who are focused on managing can never get themselves to focus on what Dr Juran calls the 'diagnostic journey' of any improvement process. Not because they are unwilling, but because their reporting structures, performance-incentives, job-roles, output standards as well as the training they are likely to have received, all taken together, do not encourage improvement.

The history of business organizations is full of cases where bright and accomplished managers were so caught up in *maintaining* their department's or division's performance levels that they completely ignored the trends that were sweeping their markets or the industry that they operated in.

Storied companies from around the world with names, such as Agfa, Eastman Kodak, Polaroid, Blockbuster, Sony's Betamax,

Sun Microsystems and many more, were all blindsided by their focus on maintaining control even as their consumers' preferences, the available technologies and new entrants in their preferred markets were rapidly changing the overall business topography.

So while maintaining things in organizations is essential to keep key parameters in a state of steady equilibrium, maintaining the status quo is obviously not enough to ensure the longevity, the financial health or the success of organizations.

The focus of managing is to look for deviations from the norm. The norm could be set based on financial or operational targets, historical trends, market forces, regulatory norms, technology limitations and so on. Managerial attention and the deployment of resources are then aligned with *looking for* and *correcting* deviations from these preset values.

Good managers are excellent at this role.

Steady States Are Reassuring

Maintaining the status quo and ensuring compliance with desirable standards is essential for humanity to go about their lives with safety and with a sense of assured well-being.

For instance, we all need to be confident that the medicines we buy from the drug stores actually contain the compounds that are meant to help our bodies treat diseases when ingested in the required doses. We need our cars to perform safely and as claimed by the manufacturers. The food that we buy and consume must not be harmful or toxic. The toys that we give to our children to play with must be safe for them. They must also conform to the stringent toy safety standards that have been laid out and accepted by regulators for the industry.

In fact, every single aspect of our lives relies on the assurance of quality standards and norms for products as well as services. Dr Juran often said that we all live behind 'quality dykes' and any breach in any of these myriad dykes can 'flood' us with consequences that could be detrimental to human life and which could place a heavy burden on societies for both the short and the long terms.

The proliferation of regulators and inspecting agencies around the world that monitor the quality of products and services based on established metrics and standards is an indication of how critical this *assurance* is for society.

Any adverse deviation—discovered by regulators or on account of negative customer feedback or even an unfortunate accident—can be the cause of widespread recalls of products causing significant financial losses to the manufacturers as well as serious, and often irreparable, dents to their reputations. As we write this, Nestlé in India has had to spend considerable sums of money to restore its reputation and credibility within the Indian market because the Food Safety and Standards Authority of India (FSSAI) had found that their two-minute noodles contained more than the permissible micro-levels of lead. A few thousand kilometres away, both in Europe and the USA, Volkswagen cars were being recalled because of embedded software that management had deliberately introduced into the vehicles so as to 'disguise' the actual emissions of the engine, making it seem as if the engines were compliant with the stringent emission standards of the European Union (EU) when in reality they were not.

The need for maintaining and upholding standards covers almost all aspects of human and societal interactions. Anyone who provides goods or services—whether free of charge or on payment—has a duty to ensure that the key metrics that ensure the satisfaction of those who are intended to be served are sustained. This in turn happens when committed people—good, ethical managers—ensure that they use all the resources at their command to achieve these requirements at all times.

Why Improvement Is Inevitable

Organizations need to innovate and improve. One of the reasons is that collective human expectations rise over time displaying a 'drift' towards a superior set of features or standards. Whatever new features may have excited a new car-buyer in 1980 are likely to leave him or her completely cold in 2016. The innovative designs, curves, performance standards and technologies in a new model that gave the 1980s buyers an 'Ah, ha!' and a 'Wow!' feeling then, are very unlikely to inspire the same feelings in a young 2016 buyer, when offered the very same vehicle.

Why does this happen?

There are two reasons for this. First, new generations quickly absorb the prevailing technologies or standards, and treat them as a 'given', that is, as the prevailing datum for their times. What this generation becomes comfortable with becomes the level *beyond* which all new products and services need to operate.

Second, the rate at which new ideas and concepts spread across the world today is unprecedented in the history of humankind. Thanks to the ubiquitous use of the myriad Internet communication platforms, television as well as the proliferation of mobile devices with cameras, news and information flow around the world in a matter of milliseconds. The diffusion of ideas and technologies, therefore, is occurring at powered-exponential rates.

Many of our readers, who were born after the mid-1980s, would all have grown up with computers and would definitely have had a chance to use their computers and laptops to do their homework, play computer games, download music or maps and chat or video-talk with their friends. These features form the datum level for such customers.

If a new computing device has to attract their attention, therefore, and give them a sense of wonderment, then all the features that the laptops of the pre-millennial generations had would have to be included as the expected *minimum*. Over and above that, the computing device would have to have many more innovative features which would constitute the *plus* in the features.

This trend is clearly observable in the ongoing race for market share among mobile device manufacturers. The innovative features offered by an iPhone or a Samsung Galaxy become the baseline for all: not just the innovative front-runners but all other manufacturers as well. The other requirement is affordability. If the same features as the market leader can be offered at a lesser price than the leader, it would be perceived as greater value for money.

The adoption of improvements is an inevitable process within human societies. Ever since human societies moved away from being hunter-gatherers—about 15,000 years ago—and started to domesticate animals and cultivate crops that were originally collected from the wild, improvements started to happen. Agricultural techniques were perfected and the connections between the use of fertilizers and water in enhancing crop yields were established.

With the synthesis of ammonium nitrate in the nineteenth century and its widespread use to fertilize soils, agriculture has been revolutionized. With the improved availability of seeds and irrigation methods, yields have been greatly enhanced.

These rapid and transformative changes have enabled our planet to feed a large proportion of over 7 billion people who are on Earth today.

Leading: Demolishing Status-quo Thinking

Improvement requires a different set of skills, resources and processes than are required for maintaining the status quo or staying in a state of control.

It is not without reason that many of the greatest innovations and inventions of humankind have occurred on account of *rebellious thinkers*—people who consciously chose not to let the prevailing understanding of their times determine the trajectory of their own thoughts or ideas. They disregarded the predominant paradigm of their times and creatively worked to make things different *and* better.

Even today, discoveries and innovations that have been made by individuals working alone or in small teams are responsible for the betterment of human life in a variety of areas. Simultaneously, when people readily take to a new technology or product, it can often become what is known as a *game changer* because the underlying model for delivering value is completely different. The Internet is an example of a game-changing technology that completely nullified the value of a fax machine. Similarly, the automobile was a game changer for horse-drawn carriages.

Innovation often means moving completely away from what an organization might be doing currently. Many companies that wish to remain market leaders and stay ahead of the pack often engage in what is called *disruptive innovation*. The objective is to change the business model, even as competing organizations are getting comfortable producing products similar to those of the market leader. By being innovative, therefore, an enterprise can serve a need in society in ways that give it an advantage in comparison to its market adversaries.

Leaders Embrace and Stimulate Change

There are six distinct qualities of leaders that distinguish them from managers. As a mnemonic, these can be remembered as the '6Es of Outstanding Leadership'.

All the six qualities are about the relentless drive of leaders to initiate change and inspire their followers to join them on the unique journey to a 'better' state. Leaders are risk-takers and always change-ready. They might like stability for a while, but then they will forge on. Here are the six key actions that transformational leaders—committed to achieving goals that are linked to a lofty vision—will always be involved in.

1. *Exposing the possibilities and the need for change*: First of all, leaders notice and clearly identify the things that need to change for the better. They just cannot be satisfied with the *status quo*. They are imbued with an adventurous, risk-taking spirit that enables them first to question things that others take for granted or accept, and then to go to places where others just do not dare.

   Garbage on the streets, wastage in a system, unresponsive public service organizations, falling margins in products, dissatisfied customers, diminishing profits, the lack of social justice, the denudation of forests, the pollution of water bodies, the adverse effects of climate change, growing population, increasing violence against women and children, the improper behaviour of elected representatives and anything that touches the person's heart and which can be transformed to function at a better level than before, become motivating factors to arouse and galvanize leaders. Every problem is an opportunity turned inside out.

   History is full of examples of leaders who were inspired to take action against things that they found glaringly unjust, inappropriate or unacceptable. It is only because leaders believe in making change that they are able to forge ahead—often at a great emotional cost to themselves. We all know that any departure from the 'norm' or embracing new or novel ideas is often met with ridicule or opposition or both. Leaders remain unfazed in spite of such 'push-back'.

2. *Envisioning the desired future*: Leaders envision the kind of future that they wish to create. Leaders are able to 'see' with their mind's eyes what they wish to achieve by intervening in a situation. They can see the final outcome and the improved end result of the condition that needs to be changed. In that sense, they are 'visionaries' who can see what others cannot. We also believe that along with 'seeing' they *create* in their minds a vision of the desired future, which also enables them to pursue that image with vigour and zest. In fact, they possess an indomitable will to achieve their vision.

   Martin Luther King envisioned how America would be transformed without any trace of racial prejudice and segregation. He could see how the actions of his followers would change America for ever. Other great leaders from diverse walks of life and from different eras of our history, such as Joan of Arc, Mahatma Gandhi, Abraham Lincoln, Lech Walesa, Nelson Mandela, Florence Nightingale, Jamsetji Nusserwanji Tata, Guru Gobind Singh ji, Rosa Parks, Baba Amte, Vinoba Bhave and so many others from around the world, demonstrated this remarkable ability to envision the desired future.

3. *Enlisting the support and involvement of others*: Once the desired future vision is clear, committed and outcome-oriented leaders need to rally their team members—their troops—and enlist their complete involvement in the mission that has to be achieved. Leaders realize that big projects need committed and competent people to ensure that the desired vision is brought to fruition. For this, the execution of the necessary steps needs to happen flawlessly.

   Yet one cannot involve others unless they too 'buy in' to the vision and pursue the desired goals. Enlisting the support of others is a means to appeal to the quest for meaning and purpose in the hearts of all of us. Leaders, therefore, know that this is an exercise in communicating the vision, so that the followers too can clearly see what the leader has already seen. Only then will the followers stand committed.

   A very simple but elegant story reveals the power of enlisting others.

   Two masons were working on two ends of what seemed to be an ordinary brick wall. However, one of the masons despite his competence was doing a shabby job of brick-laying while the other one, with no more skill than his colleagues, seemed to be working faster and doing a much better job. After everything seemed to fail, when it came to motivating the former mason to do a better job, the supervisor chose to inquire from him whether he knew how important it was to do his job with greater care and speed.

'Have you any idea how important it is that the wall that you are making is without flaws?' the supervisor asked.
'You must be joking,' the mason replied. 'Nobody wastes time or energy into making a boundary wall!'

When the same question was put to the better mason, he answered:

'Sure I know! It isn't often that a person gets a chance to build the main wall of one of the most magnificent temples of this region!'

In the second man's answer lay the secret of his commitment: He was fired by the power of the vision that somebody had cared to share with him. By knowing that he was contributing to something 'larger than life' he was inspired in his work.

Communicating the larger vision is not only about sharing the information but also about conveying the conviction and the faith that the leader has, that the vision is verily that of a better place to be. It is also a way of tagging the hopes and dreams of people to the vision, so that they are self-driven from that moment onwards. People believe the leader, because he or she communicates with confidence and shows evidence of being trustworthy.

4. *Empowering people*: Empowerment is the opposite of helplessness. When people are helpless they cannot do much, let alone pursue big, audacious and transformational goals.

Empowered persons do not feel incapable of doing the things that need to be done for the overall betterment of their organization or their enterprise. They do not let constraints on the outside limit them. They are accountable and autonomous, and demonstrate courage over caution. They operate from an inner conviction and pursue greatness rather than the routine work.

Obviously, a person who focuses on the 'I factors' (see the Section 'Choice and Accountability' in Chapter 1) is likely to be more inclined to be a self-starter than the one who is not. But leaders play a critical role in ensuring that such people are supported and their autonomy is encouraged and reinforced, so that they can take even bigger and bolder steps when needed.

Leaders make their followers and team members feel powerful by helping them to be and function autonomously and to create a space and an atmosphere where followers who are inspired to work towards the vision are encouraged and given more authority. The beauty is that, the more the leader shares 'power' and authority, the more empowered the team feels and the greater is the movement towards the vision.

5. *Exemplifying by personal action*: The phrase 'walk the talk' has become rather common in the context of leadership to demonstrate that leaders need to do as they say. They have to keep their word and make promises only when they know that they will be able to honour them, in spite of changes that might occur in conditions around them. This quality of being able to do as one wishes others to do as well is a critical component of effective leadership. It inspires followers to reach the lofty heights that leaders say they can achieve, especially if they do—with the leader—what he or she says they must.

The credibility of leaders is a function of how they are perceived by the people who have reposed trust in their leaders. If leaders say something and then do something contrary to that they will never be trusted. They would, in fact, no longer have the influence that they may have commanded.

The values and vision that drive leaders towards their goals have the power to become the guiding lodestone for the followers as well. This is why it is essential for leaders to exemplify these values through personal action. And then follow them consistently and without exception the credo that has been communicated.

6. *Encouraging the actions of others*: Whenever a leader envisions lofty goals and then inspires and enlists his or her followers to

achieving them together with him or her, the leader is also sending out a clear signal that the goal will be achieved together as long as we traverse the task together and work cohesively.

A leader appreciates that the tasks involved in bringing the vision to fruition require not just the active involvement of the entire group but also their negotiating and working through some arduous and difficult terrain.

Leaders also know that the only other source of joy for their people—apart from the happiness derived from pursuing the challenging vision itself—is the concern that they show for their followers and the genuine appreciation that they shower on the followers for the contributions made to bring the vision to fruition.

Many have this mistaken impression that people can be made to work with passion and zeal only with money. Such people misunderstand the immense power of recognition, encouragement and engagement.

The world's most effective leaders know the positive power that encouragement has and use it appropriately and genuinely with their followers to ensure that common goals are achieved.

SIMPLE STARTING STRATEGIES

The World of Work

✓ Make a list of your unique capabilities—your skills, knowledge, competencies and preferences—that uniquely define how you would like to serve society.

✓ Determine what kind of work gives you the most joy, excitement and enthusiasm. Make a list of professions that would enable you to deploy your unique strengths and capabilities.

✓ Add meaning to your life even if the job does not provide that currently, by volunteering your time in areas that you would enjoy.

✓ Join a professional organization that provides a chance for fellowship and developing your leadership skills.

✓ At your place of work become a part of an improvement team and try and make things better. Be a good follower/ team member.

✓ In your community, engage with the resident welfare association and use your spare time to make your neighbourhood garbage-free.

✓ Teach young boys and girls about sustainability and recycling of trash.

✓ Take up a hobby that helps you to use your technical skills to help society.

(B) Queries and Responses for Chapter 3

What are the skills needed by professionals who wish to succeed in the real world?
Professionals obviously need to be proficient with the domain knowledge that they are expected to have expertise in. They could enhance their chances of being called to deploy their capabilities if they also have relevant experience, a good track record of delivering results and the ability to express their thoughts and ideas effectively. Finally, as we have mentioned elsewhere in this chapter, effective people have to be change-ready at all times and be willing to initiate and make improvements.

The other skills they need to have are the ability to get along and work with others so that the goals of the business are accomplished. They have to be able to be effective in the role of a 'manager', and make plans, set targets, deploy resources and personnel and lay down procedures and standards to achieve the desired results. Simultaneously, they have to be good leaders too, with a high degree of emotional intelligence and concern for the people whom they work with. Good professionals also need to be able to communicate the overall goals to the entire team, enlisting their involvement and support for the larger organization.

In the course of their engagement, professionals will also need to be receptive to the issues of the groups that they work with. They need to listen actively to feedback that they receive from those on the front line of the activities. They must give feedback and directions, and thereby cultivate stronger teamwork and positive rapport and relationships at all levels.

Finally, an openness to learn is also an essential requirement. Professionals who are effective understand that innovations in technology, materials, processes, skills and procedures can dramatically alter the way businesses are run. They appreciate that obsolescence rates are high and the only way to remain effective is to be a step ahead of changes through continuous learning.

It also helps professionals to have a positive attitude and outlook towards life generally, which contributes to the continuous and systematic improvement of the essential skills needed to succeed.

What matters more in a professional setting—a job that is challenging or one that is just high on earnings?
This question is best answered by you because it does depend on what you consider important. In our experience the challenging jobs are the ones that bring the best out of you and prepare you for dealing with complex problems in diverse spheres. That also assures good earnings.

A job that is low on challenge might pay well—but we think such jobs are disappearing fast (if they have not already!). Nobody—including government organizations—will pay someone good money unless that person brings considerably more value to the organization that is being paid out.

From a 'quality of life' perspective, your ability to earn will influence the kind of creature comforts you can afford. But even the definition of what is 'comfortable' varies from one individual to another. What might be comfortable for you could be a necessity for another. The bottom line is: You decide for yourself and face the outcomes of your choice boldly.

Academic institutions including schools of business do not seem to be preparing us to apply the concepts that are taught to us. This is especially so for those who wish to start their own businesses. Where can one gain practical insights?
Most academic courses are designed to give you a broad foundation of essential knowledge, concepts and skills that can help you to navigate through life in a purposeful way. However, the complex manner in which societies evolve, alongside the rapid advances in science, technology, engineering, medicine, culture and arts, makes it impossible for academic institutions to ever keep pace with *all* the skills and knowledge that a person needs throughout one's life. So, we have to appreciate that life requires us to be continuous learners.

Practical insights can be gained from the experiences of others who may have traversed the path that you are intending to be on. However, we are of the view that each individual's learning must happen through the individual's own experiences—since no two persons are alike, and even when they are traversing the same pathway, they can have very different experiences.

For setting up one's own enterprise or a start-up, there are a number of societies that have been created by entrepreneurs themselves. These bodies often have workshops and seminars for the benefit of budding entrepreneurs. It would be a good idea to associate with some of these bodies for specific guidance. One might even find a successful business leader in such an outfit, who might wish to mentor you on your journey. Finally, in this age of massive open online courses (MOOCs) many reputed academic organizations offer specific and targeted online programmes for budding entrepreneurs.

Will I be successful as a trainer/facilitator in the training and development space?

If you are committed to becoming an effective trainer/facilitator and you believe that you can make a positive difference in the development of people, then—with the sharpening of the requisite skills—there is no reason for you not to succeed.

One needs to appreciate that facilitating the learning of adults requires a set of competencies that are different from those that, say, school teachers have. The principles of adult learning apply to adult learners and you would need familiarity with those principles and a deep knowledge of their application. Furthermore, to be an exemplary trainer of adults, apart from being effective in the learning setting, you need to display consistent evidence of the following traits:

1. Responsiveness to learner needs
2. High energy levels and enthusiasm
3. Humour
4. Authenticity and genuineness
5. Flexibility
6. Tolerance

How can I bring a change in my outlook so as to 'gel with' and build rapport with my peers at the workplace?

The only place where meaningful change can occur—especially the kind that is lasting and which you alone can control—is within yourself. Our 'outlook'—the way we look out at people, places, events and situations—determines how we perceive others.

Perceptions play a big role in influencing our responses and behaviours. As has been shared in earlier sections of this book, our perceptions are clouded by past experiences, assumptions we make and our conditioned beliefs and values.

To gel with others requires you to interact and engage with people in ways that are warm, friendly and respectful. Many times we hesitate to take an initiative in matters such as this because we are concerned about the manner in which others might respond to our overtures. Remember that the stimulus—how others react to you—is beyond our control. If this is coming in the way of how we interact, then we need to change our response and the associated feelings so that we are not limited by our own thinking. As has been explained, we can question, revisit and transform our own thinking, beliefs and assumptions to feel good after most interactions. Often the heartburn or the lack of rapport is triggered by the expectations that we have of our interactions.

That said, you might do all that you can to build rapport with your peers at the workplace, yet you may not receive the warmth or the friendly comradeship that you expect. That should not deter you. You continue to do your bit—with a positive outlook but with few expectations. If something good emerges through your persistence that would be a bonus and you'll feel good.

Before entering the workforce or joining a company there would be some things that we would need to learn. What are the skills to have before starting one's career?
The fact that this thought has crossed your mind is appreciated.

Having a learning orientation and an openness to acquire the knowledge and the skills to be effective are essential to have throughout one's life, but definitely at the start of one's working career.

You would also need to have a degree of proficiency with the domain knowledge that you would require for your role in the company you join. But that would not be all. You would need the skills that would enable you to communicate with others, work harmoniously in teams, galvanize your subordinates to higher levels of performance, get along with people from diverse cultures and maintain a balance between the varied demands of people in your life.

That is where the skills and insights that this book provides fit in with these other imperatives.

How can one manage one's work with the demands of personal life and having a family? Is it possible to balance the two?

Yes, bringing in balance between conflicting requirements and expectations in life is possible. In fact, learning how to balance the diverse expectations of those in touch with you is a life skill that needs to be mastered early in life.

What this imperative really boils down to is figuring out your priorities in life. You will find many people who boast of having a very successful career and who, thereby, have created huge bank balances and material assets for themselves. They definitely have achieved what they had set out to do because that was a priority for them, and they made choices accordingly. Maybe they had consciously given a lower priority to their personal roles and responsibilities. For many others, their family and the well-being of their children and parents are a priority. They make their choices accordingly and are content with the outcomes that they create.

If you wish to have a healthy balance between your professional and personal lives, you would need to make your choices that are in alignment with this desire.

As I am about to embark upon a career in the corporate sector, I am spending considerable time agonizing on the idea whether I will be able to adjust to that environment or not.

Joining any new corporate organization will mean a new environment and a new set of people to interact with. Any and every one experiences a degree of anxiety as one enters into a new job, a new place or a new relationship. That's because you have never been in that space before. The territory is unknown, the people are not familiar and even the work is going to be new. Besides, there are no maps that can uniquely guide you. You will, therefore, have to make adjustments to be happy and productive.

It is good to give yourself enough time to settle in. It will take time to understand the organizational culture, the values that guide behaviour as well as the firm's vision and immediate goals. You will have to work on the understanding that you are likely to be immersed into activity and work assignments right from day one.

You may need to do some reading every evening, after work, till you become familiar with the processes, procedures as well as the norms and the culture of the organization.

The organization may have a mentoring programme in place. If a senior executive is assigned to mentor you, feel free to make the most of this resource. A senior colleague can be an able friend to guide you as you get acquainted with your organization and your role as a professional.

Should we view our work colleagues as friends, competitors or just individuals?

In the workplace there is a natural tendency to consider colleagues as competition. That's because the system, the structure and the culture of most organizations do stimulate rivalry between peers. If the one 'prize' for a group of peers at the end of a cycle of appraisals is attractive and coveted by all, it can cause an intense contest that can become quite bitter. If the organization wishes such a clash between peers, that too is fine.

What you need to appreciate, however, is that irrespective of the fact that the culture of many organizations encourages peer-to-peer rivalry, all good work that organizations do happens through teamwork and collaboration.

As you start working together, despite the culture and the factors that are used to appraise employees, there will be a number of friendships that will be made and nurtured at an individual level. Some relationships would grow despite the rivalry, and the sense of intense competition will reduce. However, many of your colleagues might be indifferent to you and would interact with you only when work requirements force them to. It would be fine to treat such people as 'individuals' if you like and if that makes you happy.

If the company—as a policy—wishes to minimize team rivalry then its systems and processes related to 'rewards and recognition' might need to clearly define the criteria on the basis of which the 'prize' will be given. If the rules are salient and are followed meticulously as announced then the emerging clarity can prevent an unhealthy undercurrent of competition. You can then treat your work colleagues as friends.

How may I deal with situations when my boss suggests a wrong approach to an issue? Is it right to give him or her advice? Also, if my superior comes up with an idea that I think may not work, what should I do?

First of all you have to have a valid reason—and some facts and data—to support your view that your boss may not be suggesting a viable solution to a specific problem. That way, it is not just an opinion that you are putting forward but a well-thought-out case in your support. That is far more convincing—not just to your boss but even to your colleagues and peers, especially if you are trying to suggest a way that seems different from what others might have considered.

With respect to your boss, if you are certain that you have some other better approach to solving an issue as compared to your superior, then please do share it. However, let your motivation to offer your solution be to solve the problem in the most optimal fashion, rather than to 'show down' your boss in the meeting.

What might help you to present your ideas objectively would be the PREP formula. 'P' stands for the alternative proposition that you state, followed by the reasons 'R'—including facts and data—that you have put together by way of evidence to opt for 'P'. The 'E' stands for not just the evidence in support of 'R' but also examples where the proposed idea (the last 'P') has worked. Following the PREP approach would help in communicating your suggestion to your boss without him/her or anyone else feeling 'downed'. Your idea may still not get accepted; however, you will feel good that you did not just keep it to yourself, but put it forward.

Should I focus on my personal performance rather than the performance of the team that I am on?

The relevance and the reasons for a team to exist are to multiply the efforts put in by each member of the team. Furthermore, effective teams are designed with clarity about the team's goals, the roles of each member as well as the right processes and the norms that need to be in place. Not only that, before the team sets about its tasks, the members are all put through an orientation process, so that the team is collectively primed for success.

Good team design ensures that when individual team members give their best for the accomplishment of the tasks—within the team's norms and processes—the collective output and performance of the team are also of a superlative order. That is how the goals of the organization are achieved.

Obviously, the short answer to your question, therefore, is that you focus on giving your best performance which is aligned with the goals of the team. Hopefully, the team is well designed and, hence, your individual effort will count for a lot.

Throughout the organization, the synergy and collaboration of high-performing teams is essential to accomplish organizational goals. Personal performance has to be in line with the overall direction of the team one is on. Also, the alignment of the independent pieces of a puzzle is necessary to create and achieve the overall picture. As in the Kerala long-boat races, each and every boatman has to row in the same direction to reach the finish line first. So your personal performance has to blend with the team performance to reach the finish line.

How should I make myself visible to my superiors in the work context?

When you use the phrase 'making [yourself] visible' do you wish to be taken notice of by your superiors for the professionalism that you bring to the job? Or is it the desire to be liked and loved by people in your organization for all the funny 'antics' that you do at the workplace?

We think that you mean making yourself 'visible' in a positive way where you are noticed for the good work that you do.

Obviously, given that making yourself 'visible' is important to you, we suggest that you pursue a systematic strategy of making your work results visible to your boss and other key superiors. To do this you need to excel at whatever tasks have been assigned to you, and do them professionally, within budget and on time.

If you are able to accomplish the tasks so that:

* There are no cost overruns,
* You get the approbation of your customers/stakeholders for the work accomplished,
* Your team is involved and they too get credit—from you and your superiors—for their efforts in the overall set of tasks,

- There is evidence of potential benefits that accrue to the firm due to the overall effort and, finally,
- You achieve the tasks in a spirit of collaborative accomplishment, and not by confrontation.

then you would be on the right track to be noticed in a wholesome and exemplary way.

In the course of your work if you take care of the above-mentioned five points and demonstrate consistent positive results, then you may further embellish your credentials by networking with people within the organization. Networking and reaching out to other decision-makers and colleagues—even those who may not be part of your function in the enterprise—help to create a supportive 'constituency' that you can rely upon whenever needed. Participate in events and functions that your firm organizes and to which you are invited. Use the chance to acquaint yourself to others.

In case interacting with people and networking during events and functions is a strain, and does not come naturally to you, then focusing more on the accomplishment of business results is a better bet. This builds a positive track record and decision-makers do keep an eye open to identify and recognize high-performing employees.

I am in a team where one half is against the other. I seem to be the middleman. How can I turn the situation around?
It isn't clear what your role in the team is.

If you are just another concerned member, then you may share your perspectives with the team leader and help him or her try and ameliorate the situation. You obviously have to cultivate trust with the team leader so that he or she does not see you as a critical, 'nosey parker' trying to meddle and mess around with what is his or her responsibility.

However, if you are the team leader and are presiding over a group that is showing poor synergy and needless conflict, then you will need to take responsibility and straighten things out.

If you are just another team member whom others confide in because they find you an effective listener, an honest broker and a trustworthy 'middleman', then you may need to play that role too. With the trust of both sides, you may be able to defuse the conflict by having both sides understand the importance of collaboration.

A word of caution is in order at this point: Such a non-formal role may make you feel good, but there is a risk that you may run out of patience if the two conflicting sides do not heed your advice. You may also feel emotionally drained, impatient and tired by your honest efforts at mediation. You, therefore, need to take a call and decide whether you really do need to get into that role at all.

Is it true that work takes so much of one's time that to expect a balance between life and work is impossible?
The kind of work that one does and the domain one functions in influence the time and the effort one has to put into one's job to be productive and effective. Yet, the truth also is that most knowledge workers who depend on their brains to be capable and effective cannot expect their brains to function indefinitely.

Our brains need rest. Even if we try and use our brains beyond eight or nine hours at a time it will still shut off. You may still be at the workplace, but your output would be low until such a time that the mind feels rested and rejuvenated.

In today's metropolitan cities considerable time is also spent commuting from your place of stay to that of work. To an extent the flexibility that many employers provide—of working from home—is an effective way to deal with this additional burden.

To be able to work productively and in a manner that is good for one's mental and emotional health requires us to understand that our bodies and minds are not machines that can be run indefinitely. Rest is imperative for our long-term well-being. Even while working it helps to be mindful and be present in the 'now'.

It is not impossible to maintain a healthy balance between the rigours of work and the requirements of rest and relaxation. It starts with the right approach to both and ensuring that you take on work in 'packets' that can be done while alternating with periods of rest and relaxation. It also requires that you do not keep long hours at work just to 'look good', to 'leave after the boss' or generally to 'keep up with colleagues'. In such situations you rob yourself of the rejuvenating time that you can spend with your family, spouse, children or pets. At other times, the workload may genuinely be higher than normal. Even then, it helps to determine an appropriate approach that enables balance to be maintained.

At the workplace, is it better to be a good communicator or be a technically sound manager?
The way this question has been asked, one would think that 'good communication skills' are a substitute for technical skills or domain knowledge. One cannot replace the other. However, both are needed to be effective in any role. The ability to convey one's ideas, decisions and opinions effectively, along with a thorough understanding of the 'technical aspects' of the job are together required to perform any role effectively. In fact, being good at communicating ideas that are rooted in domain-specific knowledge and experience and that are relevant to the task assigned is a 'mantra' for success.

As with any other set of skills, working regularly to deepen one's domain expertise, as well as one's communication ability, while honing any weaknesses in either area will provide a sturdy foundation on which a manager can build a robust career.

As a manager I am expected to know the people in my team. Is it appropriate to keep in touch with them—in a friendly way—just to get to know them better, and facilitate harmonious working?
Working with your team in a way that fosters goodwill and harmony among all the members is always a good outcome to pursue. The team's effectiveness and performance levels are bound to be better if such an investment is made. However, how much time you can actually spend with the team and how often would depend on the number of people in your team. If you have about five to seven direct reports, there is merit in investing time in the team's development and encouraging bonding that goes beyond the workplace as well. With a large number of people working below your direct reports, an 'all hands meeting' once in a few months helps to bring all on board, especially when you share the goals of the organization and elicit feedback in a positive, non-threatening atmosphere. Many good ideas and suggestions can be garnered from such interactive meetings, which also help to forge wholesome ties among the team members and defuse any potential irritants and conflicts that can adversely affect performance.

The frequency and the quality of the interactions must be such that it is seen as a professional exchange. It should not devolve into an intimate 'carping session' where the absent superiors are excoriated or verbally 'dragged over hot coals'. Keeping that professional distance and not encouraging critical carping is appropriate.

Often one's superior carries a negative first-impression about a colleague. If I am that colleague, how can I change this situation?
The often repeated phrase 'the first impression is the last impression' is rather overrated.

There is no denying that the initial interactions between people—across the table, over the phone or even through a video-chat—will convey significant cues for the other side to form impressions. During some of your early interactions, it is quite likely that your superior received or picked up some aspects of your verbal as well as non-verbal behaviour, which have given him or her a chance to form an unflattering impression about you. However, if the superior has not specifically told you that you lack in some specific traits, it would be inappropriate to *assume* that your senior colleague harbours a negative impression about you. Very often the assumption itself is erroneous. (See the Section 'Thinking, Feeling and Behaving'.)

In India where hierarchy and respect for seniors are an important part of our cultural upbringing, many people find it difficult to openly communicate with their seniors. Some are visibly nervous and might even miss out on conveying what is essential. Sensitive seniors also realise this and would make efforts to ensure that the junior colleague feels at ease during the interaction.

To correct an erroneous impression that your senior may have about you, asking him/her directly how you can improve your performance/behaviour or those traits that the manager finds inappropriate or offensive always helps. Armed with this feedback, you can start working on the identified deficiencies. It would also enable superiors to change their impressions about you if you share with the person that you are wilfully working on yourself to make improvements.

When someone in our organization has a personal or family issue that affects where or how they work, the HR department is often entrusted the task of determining a solution that works best for the concerned employee and the firm. But often a

satisfactory solution is not forthcoming. What can be done in such a situation?

It is quite natural that some unplanned or unexpected things can occur at the personal level—an illness, bereavement, the start of litigation, a family dispute or whatever else, and all these may cause considerable disruption in one's life or work. These events may also trigger a need for changes in your professional set-up. For instance, relocation may be needed or one may need to move into a role where travel for work is limited.

Progressive, compassionate and humane employers and organizations would certainly wish to find a solution that works for the enterprise as well as the affected employee. Obviously, a lot depends on how 'senior' and 'valuable' the employee is to the organization, and how many years the person has served the firm. But irrespective of these factors, a function such as the human resources (HR) is likely to be entrusted the task of determining the best way forward.

It helps if the affected employees can clearly articulate what they want of the enterprise. It is good to present one's ideas in writing. Meeting the highest authority in the organization to present your perspective is also a good idea, especially in owner-run organizations. HR can then ascertain how best to achieve that goal without too much disruption to the organization and make their suggestions to the head of the function. You would be satisfied that you have made your case strongly.

The real world obviously is not like a machine where a given situation will elicit a precise and specific response. Despite the best efforts of all concerned in the organization, it is very likely that not all conditions—that would make life easy for the affected employee—can be worked out satisfactorily. In the event this happens, and after all other creative possibilities have been exhausted, it might be necessary for the employee to make an informed choice—and take a decision that might also require leaving the firm.

Feeling bitter about the firm or the HR department will only aggravate your misery and is not the response of someone who wishes to be accountable. In fact, you should be glad that you left no stone unturned in expressing what you wanted. The results may not have been the way you wanted, but you should be satisfied that you did try.

When life throws a person the equivalent of an unexpected googly, one can easily lapse into a state of self-pity, especially if one is not mindful and chooses to mope. One has to avoid this and move ahead with a positive, action orientation. If the organization one works for is able to help, then one should give thanks and move on. If not, even then one should give thanks and move on focusing on the thought that there will be other opportunities and solutions that are bound to emerge sooner than later.

What should I do if I have to fire an employee of my department?
We presume that by the phrase 'firing someone' you imply the dismissal of an employee from service.

The first thing one has to do is ascertain if the person being fired is being let go of because of a restructuring in your department or because of some performance or behavioural issues. The reason why this needs to be clear at the very beginning is to be able to craft your message to the outgoing employee accordingly.

The second part involves following the appropriate process for terminating the services of an employee. Involuntary termination of an employee—who has been found committing an offense—can only happen after the laid-down process of taking 'disciplinary action' has been completed. Every organization has a well-laid-down system and a set of procedures that have to be followed before an employee can be dismissed.

If the employee is being 'laid off' as against being dismissed, then the employee might be eligible for certain benefits and pay-outs that would have been worked out beforehand. However, the situation would be quite different for someone who has violated company policy and breached a written or tacit compact that exists between the employee and the organization.

When a person is found guilty of a minor or a major violation, the elements of natural justice need to be followed, even as disciplinary action is being taken. What this means is that well before the initiation of a person's dismissal from the organization for any transgression, the employee has to have been given ample opportunities to explain ('show cause') why his or her offense should not be punished. Furthermore, the employee may also have to be given a chance to atone, make commitments to reform and demonstrate good behaviour within the organization in future. It is obvious that in such situations firing the employee will have to wait. If there is another infringement by the employee, the disciplinary process has to be followed afresh.

There are certain infractions, though, for which the organization might have a policy of 'zero tolerance' or 'firing after a warning for the first offense'. Theft, sexual misconduct involving a colleague, harassment of women, abuse of authority and the like are some of the offenses and contraventions of policy that are written down as part of the firm's code and which can elicit summary punishment of the perpetrator. In such situations the employee is often given a chance to resign from the services of the company voluntarily or face disciplinary action.

When a person has done thorough work, he or she is not receptive to any negative feedback. How do you work around this situation, especially when there is a need to point out some deficiencies?

If someone has worked hard at doing a job well, that person—quite rightly—expects appreciation first. However, many of us have the habit of ignoring the enormous amount of good someone has done and focusing only on the small errors that may have occurred in the course of accomplishing the major job. If this is how we have been behaving—and our colleagues know about this tendency of yours to 'minimize the good' and 'maximize the bad'—then their receptivity for your feedback will be low.

Instead, if you genuinely show appreciation for the 'thorough' work done by your colleague and then point out—objectively—what improvements can be kept in mind for the next time, you are bound to see that your colleague will be more receptive to feedback thereafter.

PART II

Additional Guidance Questions

4

Queries and Responses

(A) Making Impactful Presentations

How does one get a free flow of words during a presentation? Does that completely depend on vocabulary, or does it have something to do with preparedness?
Most definitely, the command and control on one's language has a huge role to play in delivering a smooth, uninterrupted presentation. The good news is that one can consistently work on and improve one's vocabulary. It is a dynamic process. Reading and listening to pieces which are well drafted and have a powerful and appropriate usage of words is a good way to start.

Once a certain word comes up, and you get its meaning, make it a part of your conversations. This will help in familiarizing yourself with new words. That said, preparation and doing your homework prior to standing up to speak before an audience is a critical aspect of making fluent and impactful presentations.

What good is a treasure trove of impressive words if their usage is likely to be haphazard and slovenly? Researching your topic, sequencing the main content and body of your presentation and rehearsing your piece are essential components of preparation that—if well done—can enhance the fluency and the impact of what you say. Therefore, a robust vocabulary and preparation are both essential.

For many professionals in India, English is not their first language. In fact, most of us read/write and speak in at least three different languages, all of which are learned at different points in time. Our mother tongue comes first, then Hindi and finally English. So being fluent and effective in all three is a difficult task, but definitely not impossible.

We generally think in our mother tongue and then translate our thoughts into English. So accepting this needs to be kept in mind. Also, giving oneself the requisite time to practice and become comfortable is essential.

What is important in a presentation—content or the way the presentation is delivered?

Presentations have three main variables to focus on: the verbal, the visual and the vocal. The verbal focuses on choice of word, the main content, structuring of the presentation and the adequacy of material. This is most definitely vital. But more than this is the ability to deliver the content, in a powerful and impactful way. The speaker has to be aware about all delivery components, the visual or the body language and the vocal/voice attributes.

Body language takes care of the eye contact, the body posture, gestures, facial expressions, and body movement. The vocal strength is based on volume, pace, intonation, pronunciation and avoidance of fillers (*aaa…*, *you see…*, *I mean…*, etc.). Thorough preparation and regular practice are the key components for an effective presentation. You may also wish to revisit the Section "Communication and Building Relationships'.

How do I organize my content or thoughts when I have to speak as an extempore speaker, or write a quick essay?

If you have even a faint inkling that you will be asked to speak, do keep a few thoughts or ideas in mind from before. But if you are truly asked to speak extempore, then you will really have to think 'on your feet' as you are approaching the podium.

Winston Churchill was invited as a guest to an event. He was not meant to address the gathering. But as it happens, many people entreated him to come up on stage and share his thoughts.

He agreed to do so, and as always, he spoke brilliantly and kept his audience spell-bound. After the event when someone asked him how he did such a wonderful job without preparing, his reply was very apt. He shared that whenever he is invited to a function he comes prepared. 'What if I am requested to share my insights?' he said.

Being 'ready' and ever 'set-to-go' was his principle. This is good advice.

For writing an essay or speaking extempore, organizing one's thoughts involves a few basic steps:

1. Have the objective of the presentation clearly spelled out: A one-line objective that defines the main takeaway from the written piece or the spoken presentation.
2. Start reflecting and collating your own thoughts that fit the objective: Choose the ideas that you can confidently speak about.
3. Plan the sequence in which you will use the ideas that you have chosen.
4. Start with the first idea and ensure that the other thoughts follow in a smooth sequence.
5. Wrap up with a conclusion that demonstrates to the audience (and yourself) that the objective of your talk was achieved.

How can I present my thoughts in front of a group of people? How can I get better at this?

Presenting one's thoughts/ideas in front of an audience is a skill that can be improved easily and systematically with due preparation and practice.

The more you take up opportunities to stand up and speak to an audience, even though you feel nervous initially, the more confident you become.

Preparing prior to delivering your speech to a group is essential. Here are a few pointers to make the process effective:

1. Have the objective of your presentation clearly spelled out. A one-line objective that defines the main goal of your speech should be crafted.
2. Start collecting, researching and compiling the material that fits in with your communication objective. Keep in mind that

simply collecting material without developing a proper structure would be meaningless.

3. Plan the sequence of your speech. The beginning/introduction, the main body and the closing should be determined next. The structure and the sequence need to have a smooth flow. It helps to be logical and makes the structure easy to follow for the audience. An unstructured, rambling talk would be difficult for the audience to either understand or concentrate upon. You may be speaking on a relevant or an interesting topic and your audience might be receptive and eager. But if you do not have a well-structured speech you may observe the ground slipping under your feet!

4. The transitions from one idea to the next need to be smooth and coherent.

The main body of your presentation can have subheadings to further categorize the content into smaller, more manageable bite-sized chunks of ideas. The entire body, however, must remain aligned with the goal of the presentation.

This is as far as formal presentations to groups are concerned. Very often, however, in the course of meetings, seminars or conferences, one needs to express oneself and there may not be time to prepare oneself in the above-suggested manner.

In such situations one needs to take care of the following:

1. Start by getting over the inertia of not speaking! More often than not, it is our own lack of confidence that prevents us from standing up and making our point.

2. We all need to appreciate that we have a right to put forth our ideas—however different or creative those may be from what the audience may have heard till then.

3. If the audience does not 'buy into' your idea or rejects it, it is to be seen as a rejection of the idea, and not you! Never take the rejection personally.

4. The manner in which the idea is shared should follow the broad principles specified for formal presentations, earlier. Your thoughts should be cogent and expressed in a way that makes them easy to comprehend.

5. Your voice must be audible to all in the audience; if you are using a microphone, make sure that you remain alert to how it is behaving.

6. Be sensitive to the audience's expectations. If the ideas that you wish to share are about something that is far removed from the theme of the meeting or the conference, ask yourself the question: 'Why am I keen to share this idea, now?' Your truthful answer to this question will guide you.

7. Finally, when in doubt, it is better to speak up, rather than feeling frustrated at not having had a chance to put your thoughts across. It helps to learn how to assertively share your thoughts when you think that it would help the discussion.

Even though I am familiar and use powerful words in my informal conversations, I seem to forget them, and how to use them while standing up and speaking to a group. How can I deal with this?

Speaking to a group is always more stress-inducing than speaking one-on-one. This is universally true. Missing and forgetting words that you are ordinarily familiar with is but natural.

A simple, yet effective way to deal with this is to note such powerful words and phrases on *index cards* which are rectangular cards, about 12 × 7 cm in size made of card paper. In a big, bold and readable font write the words and phrases so that they are easy to read while you are speaking. Use these cards when you are delivering your presentation to the audience.

This technique is used widely and is acceptable to all categories of speakers: even the best ones!

Even when I'm thoroughly prepared to present something before a large group, I go totally blank when I am actually there with the audience. How do I deal with this embarrassment?

First of all, accept this as a natural response for speakers, especially the ones who are still working on developing their public speaking skills. It is something that you can tide over with preparation and practice.

It helps to put your talking points on index cards, in the sequence in which you intend to present them. As you speak you refer to the first idea on the first card, and when all aspects of that idea have been covered you move on to the next, as the first card is removed and kept aside. This is an acceptable practice and can be used without hesitation.

If you are making your presentation using a laptop, then the content will be in front of you, on the screen. If the speech is a long one, you may even use a teleprompter (President Barack Obama loves using these!) and the entire speech will be visible to you at your pace and speed.

These devices prevent any speaker from going 'totally blank' in front of the audience.

Is it appropriate to appeal to the emotions of the audience during a presentation?

Absolutely! In fact, most well-known speeches, that have left a mark in history, have triggered an emotional response from the audience, and thereby inspired them to action.

The speech of Martin Luther King Jr. (1963) 'I have a dream', for instance, is loaded with emotional appeal. The word 'dream' is familiar to all, because we all have dreams and relate deeply at an emotional level to these 'other worldly' expectations that reside in our hearts.

Similarly, Barack Obama's message, 'We can change!' (2008) as well as John F. Kennedy's (1961) speech committing that America would place a man on the moon were both rich in emotional content, conveying the urgency to do the things that all Americans related to.

Just a word of caution: Emotions cannot be aroused in a way that they lead to damaging consequences. Adolf Hitler made speeches that aroused people but they ended up being violent and killing over six million Jews, apart from expanding the territories of the Third Reich and trampling on the rights of peace-loving people.

(B) Social and Business Etiquette

How do you ensure that you are being sensitive and caring to someone whom you have just met for the first time, and whom you wish to befriend?

You obviously appreciate the importance of being sensitive and concerned if you wish to build rapport and forge friendly relationships.

Making new acquaintances starts with initiating introductions. This requires us to share free information about ourselves, and ask questions of the others, in ways that elicit information from them. Your questions or queries should not seem like a probe or an interrogation, but rather be light-hearted conversation that encourages the other persons to freely disclose things about themselves that they consider important.

While the other person is sharing information, we must listen very attentively and with interest. Nothing communicates care and sensitivity better than being *genuinely* concerned about the things that are of importance to the other, and which he or she is sharing with you. This too is an essential element of demonstrating caring and building rapport and friendly relations.

How can I start a conversation with a lady for the first time, so as to establish a friendly relationship?

Whatever has been mentioned earlier applies here as well, with just two additional caveats.

First, interacting with the opposite sex always involves some hesitation from both sides; hence, one has to move ahead slowly, but surely, to build trust and a friendly relationship.

Second, most women disapprove of pushy men, who are uncouth and demonstrate boorish and unrefined behaviour.

Even in this day and age, when women and men are considered equally able, ladies are still appreciative of men who show care and consideration towards their needs.

Therefore, starting with a calm, composed and confident demeanour is desirable while initiating a conversation. This is far more impressive than depending on designer clothes and accessories to make an impact. Being your genuine and authentic self is also imperative, since a false, pretentious appearance will be found out sooner than later. This would undermine trust and any friendly feelings.

After the first few interactions with a lady, you will get verbal and non-verbal signals from her as to whether she is interested to be your friend. Reading these signals correctly, and checking back with her to confirm what you think she is communicating, is a good way to take the matter forward, if she is interested.

Where should one draw a line with respect to social interactions with work colleagues?

You are the best person to judge this.

In the Indian context, the workplace—where you spend at least eight to ten hours a day with your colleagues—is treated as an extension of one's family. Accordingly, there is considerable sharing of personal matters and an involvement with the life-events of colleagues (such as marriages, engagements, birthdays, baby showers and the like). Many of these celebrations occur in 'out-of-the-office' settings and foster greater social interactions among colleagues.

Sometimes, the relaxed and unsupervised ambience of such events also gives rise to situations which can be socially inappropriate. For instance, a colleague from work might—under the influence of alcohol—display excessive affection for a lady associate or share jokes that are inappropriate or generally behave in a loud and coarse manner.

Colleagues who behave in this manner have to be reprimanded formally at the workplace, since such social interactions are with office colleagues, and any improper behaviour even outside of the office can vitiate the teamwork and the overall effectiveness of the department.

If you find that people from your office continue to behave inappropriately at social gatherings, you may need to take a call and decide if you really want to be a part of them.

I wish to know about global dining etiquette, and specifically the differences in the British and the American styles of dining.

The basics of dining etiquette around the world are essentially the same. Eating food together is an essential and important part of all human cultures around the globe. While eating together, all cultures ensure that an ambience is created where all those who are partaking of a meal feel welcome and at ease. Besides, as the meal is served and eaten, the atmosphere is relaxed, which also encourages friendly conversation and warm interactions. Such meal-times have from times immemorial been used to forge royal alliances, business partnerships, marriage proposals, tribal peace and a host of other important coalitions.

For an individual, dining etiquette would involve eating in a hygienic, courteous and appropriate manner, so that those who are sitting next to you—or even across you, on the floor or the table—do not feel repulsed by your behaviour and manners. Consideration can also be shown by knowing who the host is, using the right kinds of cutlery and if eating with the hand, doing so in a way that food is not splattered around you.

As hinted earlier, food can be eaten on the floor, with a clean eating cloth or plantain leaves or even short wooden tablets placed in front of the guests. Many other cultures prefer to eat on tables, where the guests are seated on chairs around the table.

In Britain and America, formal gatherings will specify the time when the guests need to be at the venue. If the meal is a sit-down one, then the food will be served in courses—starting with a soup, a salad, an appetizer, an entrée and the dessert. Special cutlery is to be used for each course. Tea or coffee served with the dessert indicates that the meal is over.

Depending on the occasion and the intimacy of the guests with the host and the hostess, they may get a gift of flowers, wine or chocolates for the hostess. The host and hostess in turn, might also start the meal (after the guests have mingled over drinks and small portions of snacks called hors d'oeuvre) with an announcement and a prayer or a blessing.

During the meal and over conversations, the host or any of the guests might propose a toast, honouring or remembering an event or person.

The differences between American dinner-etiquette and that of the British are mainly to do with the fact that American are generally more informal and tend to make many of the 'rules of the table' less cumbersome and easy. Also, Americans cut a few pieces of food at a time, then keep the knife away and use just the fork to pick the cut morsels. And then make a few more portions. British style involves using both the knife and fork together to cut a slice or a portion from the piece of food, eat that bite and then cut another.

Is there a way to master the 'American accent' easily?
What could be a reason for you to be willing to speak with an American accent? You need to be clear about the purpose! For someone who spends many years in a different land, the way he

or she speaks the language of that region is bound to undergo some changes as the pronunciation of words improves and as the speaker's fluency with the words is enhanced. However, someone who tries to speak in a borrowed style—either to 'fit in', not stand out, or to be comprehensible—would come forth as being unnatural. Rapport cannot be built if people suspect the way you articulate your thoughts! Authenticity requires that you speak in a manner that not only best communicates your ideas but also leaves you relaxed and not strained from having to 'put on' an accent.

There is no doubt that one has to work on the right pronunciation and diction, as well as improving one's vocabulary and the use of phrases from the culture one is in. But the natural and easy way of speaking should be retained, so as not to cause stress.

Why is it so difficult to treat people as individuals and not generalize?

The human mind has the power to perceive things based on inputs that are obtained through our senses. As a result of our interactions with different individuals, our minds categorize people and place them in different 'baskets' based on their traits, their ideas, the region they come from and so on. All this happens quite automatically, because our brain—which is designed to ensure our survival—wants to safeguard our well-being by quickly determining if there is any pattern that has been recognized in the past as a dangerous one. The human mind, therefore, has a tendency to generalize and club situations and people—as well as past evaluations and events—in a web of connected ideas.

While dealing with individuals, these patterns serve as filters in our minds and colour our perception. This is why we tend to use shared ideas to describe individuals—in the process ignoring their unique qualities. These filters and blindfolds prevent us from seeing people the way they really are.

It takes considerable practice, and being consciously mindful and aware, to tide over this tendency, and look at individuals and situations just as they are. The more centred and meditative one becomes, the more one sees things exactly as they are—reflected on the pure mirror of the mind.

Is it desirable to insert a little informality and humour even in formal events?

Introducing informality into a structured, formal event is not desirable. If the event or the setting requires a serious agenda to be covered—and that too in the presence of partners, associates or dignitaries who are not part of the organization or the country—then using humour would be inappropriate.

However, if there is a soiree or a social interaction after the formal event, and the various groups are familiar with one another, and the mood is a little mellow, some light humour would be in order. However, the humour must not be politically provocative, sexist, racist or otherwise indecorous.

Humour does have a role in brightening up the spirits of people generally, and its use, therefore, is not prohibited. What is required is sensitivity on part of the event organizers to ascertain if the occasion, the place and the people present would benefit from some light banter.

(C) Cross-cultural Effectiveness

When meeting a team, comprising people of diverse nationalities and ethnicities, what would be an appropriate way to greet them?

Situations where you need to interact with people of diverse backgrounds together, in a team, are becoming more and more common. These deliberations are not confined to just the United Nations! Large globalized organizations are always looking for the right kind of talent to run their facilities, and having multicultural workforces is increasingly common.

While dealing with multicultural groups, being sensitive and aware is an essential requirement in those dealing with them. Being mindful of the group's composition and the diversity will provide significant pointers on what greeting would be appropriate for the occasion.

If a major part of the team is English-speaking, then an appropriate greeting in English—'Hello', 'Good morning' or a simple 'Welcome!'—would be in order. But if the groups consist of people from Francophone countries, or Arabs, Japanese, Germans or

Italians, you may like to learn a few phrases to greet the team, in their language. This process has become much simpler now, with mobile apps allowing you to translate phrases and sentences into many other languages merely by typing a phrase. Some applications can also 'play' the translated sentence as a speech, so that even saves you the trouble of learning anything!

Your showing some sensitivity for the team's well-being, and investing time to make them feel at ease will go a long way to create the right conditions for harmony and building rapport. You would have noticed how foreigners and expats visiting India for work or fun get into the 'namaste' gesture. And yes, we like it.

In the context of Corporate India, there is an unwritten code in professional organizations that we all adapt to the 'Western style and culture' of doing business. In the process are we not losing our authenticity? Why should we compromise?

Companies are set up and created to serve the needs of society. In this day and age, considerable business is done across borders, with markets that exist in diverse nations and cultures. No company can serve people effectively, in any part of the world, unless there is a complete understanding of the way the market functions, the issues that need to be kept in mind while interacting with customers and the like. This requires companies—and all those who work in such organizations—to be sensitive, respecting and aware about other cultures and the differences with their own.

Today's corporations also source talent from around the world. Just as one has to be sensitive while selling to clients outside, there is considerable sensitivity required within the organization too, to ensure that people from diverse backgrounds and ethnicities feel at ease while giving their best to the organization. This requires a corporate culture that is professional, supportive of diversity and devoid of any glaring cultural symbols that can be misunderstood.

The so-called 'Western style and culture' is actually a style and culture that has evolved over the past one hundred years or so, within corporate entities in the USA and the Western Europe. The 'Western style and culture' is associated with professionalism and teamwork, gender and ethnic diversity, respect for all as well as openness and trust. In such a culture, an employee's background or personal condition does not cloud the perception, as long as the person performs within the boundaries of the role that the employee is in. You would agree that the values that the Western style and culture endeavour to support are universally appropriate. In fact, as a nation India too considers these values essential for effective management and governance of organization.

By adapting to a culture of professionalism that makes employees feel comfortable, safe and productive, we are making our organization more effective at serving our customers and communities. If the workforce is from different parts of the world, and the company canteen serves cuisines of the nations where some of the employees are from, it only makes the company a sensitive, caring employer. We are not losing our authenticity or compromising on anything, in the process.

While interacting with customers or suppliers from diverse countries, what can we do to ensure that we build effective rapport, without misunderstandings?
Today's professionals—especially those who are in functions that have contact with customers, partners, associates or suppliers across a global supply chain—need to be sensitive about other cultures and be fully aware about important 'cultural dimensions' that differentiate one nation from another. Cultural dimensions typically map the orientation of people in a region or geography based on factors such as time, communications, hierarchy, space and the like. Understanding the underlying history and the values that differentiate cultures is also important. This knowledge prepares us to deal with diverse business partners.

There is another aspect. If you have relocated to another culture, then you will have to work harder to ensure that you understand the nuances of the culture you are in. Being aware that our perceptions can trigger judgemental thoughts of the new culture, as also stereotyping and generalizing, we need to be doubly cautious not to lapse into such a state. All these actions would help you to build rapport and avoid misunderstandings. It is also helpful to treat each interaction as a fresh one, with opportunities to build further on the foundation of mutuality.

However, if your client, supplier or partner is visiting you in your country, it would be your responsibility to ensure that they feel comfortable, are looked after with due sensitivity—with consideration for jet-lag, the hot weather, the food and water that would be offered to them and so on—so that their mission proceeds according to plan and achieves the intended objectives. Even making your visiting overseas guests feel at ease in your surroundings, even as they are doing business with your firm, is a powerful and effective way of building trust and a lasting relationship.

When a delegation comprising people of diverse nationalities comes to visit our firm, what kind of behaviour, by those who interact with the delegates, should serve as the norm?
Your question reveals a keen interest and sensitivity about the fact that diverse cultures need to be 'handled' differently. This is a position that demonstrates that you are looking in the right direction!

Before we get to the behavioural norms for interacting with a heterogeneous overseas group, we need to appreciate that the ways different cultures use words, non-verbal signals and gestures—with their own compatriots, and those of other ethnicities—differ widely. Acquiring some mastery over these nuances is essential, because that reduces 'cultural friction' and stimulates heightened understanding. The mastery over the nuances is achieved by knowing as much about the others as might make you conversant with the foreign culture, as well as by respecting and accepting the differences that visitors exhibit. Besides, being change-ready, adaptable, flexible and mindful are also helpful.

The basic norms for interaction emanate from this state of preparedness. The language one uses should be simple and easy to comprehend. Jargon, local clichés and slang need to be avoided. Asking questions of the others, especially if what they say is not understood, is desirable and helpful. It is much worse if one misconstrues what is being said and ends up doing something embarrassing! Gestures can easily confuse and even offend: Hence, knowing what are offensive gestures in the cultures that are represented in the group is essential. Finally, being respectful to all—without exception and not trying to play favourites—is the foundation for the right norms for communicating with diverse groups.

While working with diverse teams what can be done if the working style of the visiting team members is very different from that of professionals from the host country?

It is likely that the style of working of your foreign colleagues would be different from that of your Indian colleagues. This is a natural outcome of the different cultures that each group has grown up with. However, there is a common goal which has brought all the diverse players together, and because achieving this goal is important to all of you, it can become the foundation for determining the most effective way to work together.

Accordingly, a good way to begin with would be for all the key team players—those from abroad as well as those from the host country—to sit together and establish working norms that would ensure that the goal orientation of the group is not compromised by the cultural differences that exist. The group can also together decide on the process and the procedure by which to resolve any issues or conflicts that might come up in the course of the team's work. With such norms in place, the emphasis is placed on the task at hand; any cultural or stylistic differences that come in the way of the group's work are resolved through dialogue and discussion. Such an approach results in harmonious working, a greater appreciation of each side's perspective on the work, and prevents issues that lurk behind cross-cultural teams to simmer in the background and remain unresolved.

How can one keep the expectations of a national and a foreign boss aligned?

Working with two superiors is ordinarily tough. Working with two 'bosses' one of whom is in country and the other overseas can be doubly challenging. Even if the two are located in country, it can be tricky!

Irrespective of the role one has in the organization, a potent recipe for success is to keep your channels of communication open and transparent. Both the executives you report to must be fully aware—at all times—about the assignments you are working on, the workload you are dealing with, the resources you are using and whether you are on target and within the budget and ahead or behind the schedule. This openness will ensure that both your superiors are on the same page, and if they are talking amongst themselves (as one would expect!), they would be able to share notes and confirm where you stand.

If an unrealistic demand is placed on you by one of the bosses, which conflicts with something that the other has assigned to you, then you may have to reach out to both of them, directly and openly (even through an email) wherein you assertively communicate the constraints that are being imposed on you. You may not get them to completely agree with your perspective, but by stating your case, you might have the bosses work out a meaningful solution to your issue. Cross-cultural issues, if any, would have to be tactfully handled by you.

Do we need to completely transform ourselves to the new culture or just adapt a few things if we are moving to a new place?
Any new place implies having a new experience. Transitioning and moving to another place and another culture is a lot of fun and learning, but it is not without its challenges. People in the new place will obviously hang on to their own set of perceptions, as well as the ways in which they do things. As you are the one who has relocated and made a cross-cultural move, it becomes your responsibility to adapt. Being open and flexible are the cornerstones of making your experience a pleasant one. One needs to approach the culture of the new place with a child-like wonder. Remember, it is not a 'you versus them' situation. It is more a position where you and your friends in the new place together will bring in new insights, creative ideas and solutions, which will enrich all sides in the process.

Bibliography and Additional Resources

CBT Blog. 2013, January 7. 'Apply the Albert Ellis' 12 Irrational Beliefs and Disputing Statements to Your Thinking…'. Retrieved 21 June 2016, from http://iveronicawalsh.wordpress.com/2013/01/07/apply-the-albert-ellis-12-irrational-beliefs-and-disputing-statements-to-your-2013/

Kabat-Zinn, Jon. 2011. Lecture at the University of Dartmouth on 'The Healing Power of Mindfullness'. Retrieved 21 June 2016, from http://www.youtube.com/watch?v=_If4a-gHg_I

Newton, Claire. 2011, July. *The Five Communication Styles*. Claire Newton blog. Retrieved from http://www.clairenewton.co.za/my-articles/the-five-communication-styles.html

Powell, Alvin. 2012, February 2. *Decoding Keys to a Healthy Life*. Harvard University Gazette. Retrieved 5 July 2016, from http://news.harvard.edu/gazette/story/2012/02/decoding-keys-to-a-healthy-life/

The Brain from Top to Bottom. 'When Fear Takes the Controls'. Retrieved 21 June 2016, from http://thebrain.mcgill.ca/flash/a/a_04/a_04_p/a_04_p_peu/a_04_p_peu.html

Thum, Myrko. 'The 10 Most Inspiring Personal Development Quotes of All Time'. Retrieved 20 July 2016, from http://www.myrkothum.com/blog/

Wakhlu, Bharat. 2007. *Total Quality—Excellence through Organization-wide Transformation*, 2/e. New Delhi: S. Chand and Company Ltd.

Wakhlu, Savita Bhan. 2002. *Managing Presentations: Communicating with Impact*, 2/e. New Delhi: SAGE Publications.

www.livingwell.org.au (accessed on 16 July 2016).

http://www.swamibhoomanandatirtha.org/ (accessed on 11 July 2016).

http://www.pathwaytohappiness.com/ (accessed on 20 July 2016).

About the Authors

Bharat Wakhlu is the former Managing Director, India, for the US helicopter company, Sikorsky Aircraft Corporation (A Lockheed Martin Company). He is an engineer with degrees in management from IIM Bangalore, and INSEAD, Fontainebleau. Bharat worked with the Tata Group, in India and the US, for three decades. He joined the group as a TAS Executive. He is a Fellow of the All India Management Association and the American Society for Quality. Bharat is passionate about Leadership Development, Corporate Governance, Sustainability and Total Quality.

Savita Bhan Wakhlu is the Managing Director of her company, Jagriti Communications, which focuses on individual and organizational learning and development. She is an engineer and a certified personal/executive coach from the New York University, New York. She is also a certified cross-cultural trainer and consultant from Berlitz, USA, and a certified EQ resource from the Forum of Emotional Intelligence Learning (FEIL), India. Savita has trained and coached senior and mid-level executives in India and the US. She is also a member of the Indian Society of Training and Development.

Both Bharat and Savita are published authors, and continue to write, speak and coach on personal effectiveness, management and leadership. They can be reached through email at bswsimplify@gmail.com.